The Life and Times of
MALALA YOUSAFZAI

Anita Gaur

Published by
PRABHAT PRAKASHAN PVT. LTD.
4/19 Asaf Ali Road,
New Delhi-110 002 (INDIA)
e-mail: prabhatbooks@gmail.com

ISBN 978-93-5186-600-8
The Life and Times of
MALALA YOUSAFZAI
by Smt. Anita Gaur

Edition
2026

Paperback Price
₹ 450.00 (Rupees Four Hundred Fifry only)

Printed at
Narula Printers, Delhi

Author's Note

Malala Yousafzai is a very young, she has gone on to attain the zeniths that few are fortunate to scale at such a young age. Generally, common women, like you and me, are scared of the goons and loafers on the roads and suffer their uncivilized behaviour thinking that they are destined to suffer. This happens only because they are women and tried to change their way of life; however, there are girls like Malala in the world who have stood before the most terrible and horrendous terrorist organisation like the Taliban. Yes, we are talking about the same Taliban that attacked right in America at the World Trade Center, and the American army is struggling with it in the aftermath. The Taliban has continued to rule the roost; despite all this, this innocent girl named Malala has defeated the dreadful Taliban; she has done it at such a small age which is simply enough to surprise and at the same time unnerve us.

This was no courageous act to criticize and write, sitting in other parts of the world, against the Taliban and its barbaric rule; rather it requires grit, fortitude, determination, firmness – all the qualities that you might have when you choose to not only speak against it, but also face it in its own backyard; it could be possible only for a girl like Malala, that too at an age when other girls of her age scarce know what the world is about and how it is run. She struggled for the right to education not only for herself but for several other innocent lives; and she continues to struggle for it even now.

It was too early for any child in any country, have received such an honour as much as 16-17 years old Malala Yousufzai. She was awarded the 2014 Noble Peace Prize. In addition to her international reputation. She had been also awarded several prestigious awards. In year 2015, California-based NASA has kept a name of Asteroid 316201 as Malala.

She was shot at on 9 October 2012 by the Taliban terrorists. If you kept yourself abreast with the current affairs, you would know that the Taliban terrorist, who shot her, wrote letters repenting for his act. This girl, hailing from our neighbouring country Pakistan, is a darling of the world now; she resides in every heart. Though she lives in London for now, yet your power of sharp observation, could find her everywhere around you; she has not given up school despite all the tempests she has gone on to face. Malala now resides in the fancy world too; in poetry and stories. There is no denying the fact that she bears her name on every golden wall of our modern civilisation; she is the new offshoot for struggle against immobility.

I solemnly thank all those people who have encouraged me to undertake this work. I also thank all those who have helped me accomplish this task. I especially thank Mr. A.K. Gandhi, without whose cooperation, this book would have remained concealed in the garb of anonymity.

—Anita Gaur

Contents

Author's Note 5

1. Malala's Swat 9
2. Taliban's Sharia 34
3. Malala's Family 47
4. Malala's Resistance 63
5. Open Opposition to Taliban 98
6. Dreaded Day of 9 October 105
7. Malala in Unknown City 127
8. Beginning of a New Life 134
9. Nobel Prize Award 160

Timeline 167

1

Malala's Swat

Malala Yousafzai was born on 12 July, 1997 at Swat district in Khyber Pakhtunkhwah province of Pakistan. She hails from the tribe, Yousafzai, which is in majority in Swat Valley. Mingora (Swat) where she was born has been the centre of the Taliban. So it makes it necessary to have a glance over the background of her birthplace before we find out more about her. This would be equally essential to understand her properly.

Swat is a district as well as a charming valley located in the North West Frontier Province (NWFP) in Pakistan. It is about 160 kilometres from Islamabad. The capital of this province is Saidu Sharif; however, Mingora remains the most important town. Looking at the scenic beauty of this valley, it is also known as the Switzerland of Pakistan.

12 July is Malala Day

Swat is not adjacent to the Afghanistan border, but a lot of people of Afghan origin live here; Malala too is a child of the Afghan clan.

Swat is often compared with the Kashmir valley as far as its beauty is concerned. Spread over about 4,000 square miles, this valley is inhabited by about a 12 lakh people. Surrounded by snowcapped mountains and lush green plains lies the lifeline of Swat Valley, the Swat river. A stream which finds it mentioned in the Rigveda, a Hindu scripture. Since then this river is known as 'Suvastu'. With the passage of time, this name changed into Swat. There is a clear evidence that this area has been a site of human habitation for more than 2,000 years. The Buddhist history of this place is rich; this valley had emerged as an important centre of Buddhist education and meditation. It is believed that Lord Buddha himself toured this place and delivered his sermons to the people of the valley.

The footmarks, left behind by the Buddha, have been preserved for posterity even today. In 326 B.C., Alexander the Great arrived here during the course of his campaign and occupied it. Later, Chandragupta Maurya made it a part of the Mauryan empire.

The Swat River originates from the confluence of the Ushu and Utror rivers in Kalam. It flows for 250 kilometres before joining the Kabul River near Charsadda. It is because of the Swat River that the soil of the Swat valley is fertile and climate is so pleasant. It also plays a role in economy with its scope for irrigation and fishing. Besides, it remains a tourist attraction. Not only Pakistani, but foreigners are also attracted by the charm of this river.

The Swat River is not the only tourist place here; rather the entire valley has a large number of historical and natural places. The Swat Museum displays the historical remains, excavated from different parts of the valley, in a very systematic manner. Just near the museum is located the Butkara Dome, which belongs to the second century

A.D. Possibly, it was built by Emperor Ashok initially, and was further expanded on five different times subsequently.

Natural beauty together with tranquil and charming environment has been a source of fascination for people, right from rulers to monks and sages. Looking at this beauty, Kanishka, the well-known Buddhist ruler, shifted his capital from Peshawar to Swat. This place is also considered the place of origin of the Vajrayan Sect of Buddhism.

The Swat valley was part of the Gandhar civilisation, which was famous for its art and scripture. From here, scripture spread far and wide. At one time, this valley had as many as one thousand five hundred Buddhist domes and monasteries, of which 400 can still be found. As this place is closely connected to Afghanistan, it becomes essential for us to discuss Afghanistan too, and when we start to discuss Malala, there is no other way but to discuss the Taliban terrorists who originate from Afghanistan.

The word 'Afghanistan' signifies the 'land of Afghans'. The medieval and better known sense of 'Afghan' is 'Pashtun' or 'Pakhtun'. The origin of the term 'Afghan' is not yet clear. The period of eighteenth century is referred to as its origin, when the Pashtun tribe went on to establish a sovereign country covering the central Asian regions. The British empire endeavoured to bring Pashtun under its suzerainty under its imperialistic and expansionist policies. The British kept on trying to attain this purpose during the entire nineteenth century, but failed in their motive.

The geographical structure of Afghanistan makes it a unique place. Right since the rise of civilisation, this place has been the route traversed by different tribes. Any one aiming to reach far-east or India's forests and rivers, would have to cross valleys and hills of Afghanistan. As it is located between Asia and Europe, Arab world and south Asia, middle Asia and west Asia, this place became a source of attraction for everybody. After the Buddhist period, the Hindu kings ruled this place, which came to an end in 1023 A.D. when Mahmood Gaznavi invaded the region. After this, different Afghan tribes ruled this place in turn. The Mughals tried to bring Swat under their rule more than once, but failed in this effort. In the 1840s, the Swat tribes unified under the leadership of Abdul Gafoor, a Sufi saint, and struggled against the British, but were finally defeated. Every time, an external power sought to conquer Afghanistan for its resources, the Afghans had to face a calamity. Every time, its courageous warriors rose to fight and expelled the invaders. Standing at the crossroads of history and geography, Afghanistan is a blend of cultures, languages, dialects and tribes.

The land of Afghanistan has three geographical regions, 29 provinces, 105 towns and 15,000 villages. It may be noted that eighty percent of its population lives in villages. Ancient customs, traditions and dogmas are prevalent here. The land is rugged and underdeveloped; transportation is poor. These villages have never been under any government rule. They can be brought under control only till they are not armed but this occasion arise sooner or later. The Afghans are aggressive by nature, and are loyal only towards their families, clans and tribal groups. They are loyal only till they wish to. (As it has been done in case of Pashtuns under Zirga). These people do not feel it necessary to be loyal to any government in Kabul.

In Afghanistan, the Pashtuns have founded the most important and most numerous caste or tribal groups. The analogical terms of 'Pashtun' and 'Pakhtun' point to two unions of the tribes. These two unions or federations are Abdali or Durrani tribe of Kandahar and Ghiljai tribe of Nangarhar-Patika, who speak the Pakhtun language jointly with the eastern tribes in Pakistan. There are some tribes which fall under none of these two unions such as Afridi, Khatak, Orkazai, Vaziri and Masood; and the British identified them as hilly tribes, and called them *Pakhtun* for their administrative convenience.

Mostly, the Pashtuns are Sunnis, and they are better known as *Pashtunwali* so far as their traditions and customs are concerned. The code of conduct of this tribe comprises *Melmastia* (hosting) and *Nanavati*, under which no individual is refused shelter who comes to seek it.

The Pashtun prestige is continuously maintained through their perennial struggle for *zar* (gold), *zoru* (woman) and *zameen* (land). The inhabitants of the north and east speak Tazik Dari, Persian and Afghani languages and dialects. They are Sunnis and follow the Zamat-e-Islami. These areas also comprise Hazar and Qizilbash pertaining to the Shiites. Its eastern area was a part of Greece, and later fell under the *Kushans*, when it was influenced by the Buddhism, much evident by the massive Buddha statue at Bamiyan.

Under its imperialist policies, the British brought Kabul under its control, and maintained control over it for some time, before they decided to free it, leaving only Khyber Pass and border areas adjacent to India under its control. Later, this area came to be known as frontier administrative tribal area and North-Western Frontier Province. The

British drew the Durand line in order to include the tribes inhabiting the eastern hills of the Pashtun area, which now forms part of the frontier administered tribal area, and the North-Western Frontier Province was included in India. With independence, this area was given over to Pakistan.

When Emperor Amanullah (1919-29) came to power in Afghanistan, he brought about a social revolution, which made the women so progressive in this area that the elite women in Afghanistan started conducting themselves as if they were Europeans; this change could be seen in their dress, etiquette, speech, self-confidence and other aspects of life. However, this emperor was done to death. In 1926, the British recognized the Swat valley as a sovereign state under the command of Miyan Gul Vadud, grandson of Abdul Gafoor.

In 1933, Zaheer Shah became the ruler and Afghanistan witnessed a period of royalty for the next four decades. In 1947, Swat became a part of Pakistan, but it continued to maintain its autonomous entity under the command of Miyan Gul Vadud. This system was brought to an end in 1969, and Swat was completely merged into Pakistan.

In the year 1953, General Mohammad Daud became the prime minister. He turned to the Soviet Union for economic and military aid, and banned customs like yashmak (veil) under which the Muslim women are supposed to cover their faces. The period until 1969, Swat was known for better provisions in education, health and roads, as well as progressive laws pertaining to the environment. This tranquil area was far more progressive as compared to other areas in Pakistan. However, with Russia becoming leftist, it tried to bring Swat, the area adjoining Afghanistan, under its influence. The Marxist parties finally targeted Afghanistan and formed the People's Democratic Party of Afghanistan. It was due to its opposition that Mohammad Daud had to resign in 1963.

Later in 1973, Mohammad Daud once again seized power and declared Afghanistan, a republic. He tried to bring Soviet Union in confrontation with other Western countries. His style distanced him from the rightist factions.

And this was the precise reason why the People's Democratic Party overthrew him in 1978, in which Mohammad Daud was assassinated. However, two factions of the party, namely Khalka and Parcham, grew apart in ideology. This was the evidence of the inception of Marxism in an Islamic country as well as bondage of Afghanistan. The extremist Islamic factions clashed with the Russians, who had entered Afghanistan quite foolishly. This was how the extremist Islamic factions were born from this type of conflict, which later changed into the Taliban.

These fundamentalist Islamic leaders were against the social reforms and started an armed rebellion. By the onset of 1979, the rightist leaders Hafizullah Amin and Nur Mohammad clashed for power. The Afghan army was routed after the rebellion, and the Soviet Union sent its forces to remove Amin; and with Amin's assassination, the Soviet Union had come to have a stay in Afghanistan. In 1980, the leader of the People's Democratic Party (Parcham faction) became the leader of the country with the Soviet support. However, it intensified opposition to the Soviet army. The rebels were supplied arms and money by America, China, Pakistan, Iran and Saudi Arabia. The most terrible mistake committed by the Soviet Union was to send in the Soviet army to bring the Afghans under control. It was owing to this that several Islamic countries unitedly initiated jihad against Soviet Russia.

When the jihad was started against the Russian forces, Pakistan instructed its embassy that all those people who wish to fight for the jihad should be given visa without questioning.

In 1985, the Mujahiddin in Pakistan united against the Soviet Union, leading to the breakout of war, due to which half of Afghanistan migrated. As a consequence, Mikhail Gorbachev, the new Soviet leader, announced that he would recall his forces.

In 1986, America supplied the Mujahiddins with stinger missiles. Najibullah became the leader of the government supported by Soviet Russia. A major decision was taken in 1988 under which America, Soviet Union, Afghanistan and Pakistan entered into a peace treaty. With this, the Soviet forces retreated, but it did not improve the situation.

The Soviet forces retreated from Afghanistan in 1989, but the civil war continued. The Mujahiddins continued to struggle for removal of Najibullah. In 1991, America and Soviet Union decided to cease all aid to both factions in Afghanistan. This decision was considered a victory for the Mujahiddins, because a year later, Najibullah was removed from power. With the going back of the Soviet army, different militia groups clashed with each other for control over the government in Afghanistan. A year after the removal of Najibullah from power, Burhanuddin Rabbani of Tazik clan became the President (after the Mujahiddin faction agreed for this). In 1994, the Taliban, with dominance of Pashtuns, started to challenging the Rabbani Government, and this started the conflict.

Between 1992 and 1995, 35,000 trained fundamentalist Muslims from Middle-East, northern and eastern Africa, central Asia and Far-East fought a war against the Russian forces. Many of these had been indoctrinated in the hundreds of madrasas established by the ISI at Karachi, Pakistan. These madrasa camps became training centres for the future Islamic fundamentalists. These extremists met in these madrasas for the first time, studied together, trained together and then fought together. None of the intelligence departments paid any attention to the outcomes that could result from the coming together of these fundamentalists.

In 1996, the Taliban occupied a large part of Kabul, and enforced its fundamentalist agenda of Islam. Under it, they started prohibition on working women as well as the custom to stone criminals to death. Rabbani joined hands with the anti-Taliban Northern Alliance, which pressurized the Taliban.

In 1997, Pakistan and Saudi Arabia recognized the Taliban government, and most countries recognized Rabbani as the head of the state. It was from here that the condition of Swat and adjoining areas worsened. Two-third part of Afghanistan fell under the Taliban's control, and its power expanded. The 1998 earthquake further assisted it in expansion of its influence; this earthquake claimed thousands of lives, while shooting up unemployment and starvation. Osama bin Laden, son of a billionaire from Saudi Arabia, took advantage of this situation.

Osama encouraged the Taliban in Afghanistan; as a consequence, America conducted missile attacks on the spots suspected to be his dens. America accused that it was he who had conducted attacks on American embassies. In the year 1999, the UN imposed economic sanctions on Afghanistan to hand over Osama for trial, but this could not materialize; rather, the Taliban proved stubborn and in retaliation destroyed the Buddhist images at Bamiyan.

The Taliban issued an injunction by which it asked the minorities to keep with them some proof of identity declaring that they are non-Muslims; and Hindu women were asked to use yashmak. All this while, Ahmed Shah Masud, an anti-Talibanist, was assassinated, and the Twin Towers were attacked in America. After 9/11 attack in America, the American leadership chose to attack Taliban, resulting in the Taliban giving up the power. With this, there arose continuous conflict between the Taliban and the allied forces.

This jihad continues to be waged even today despite the passage of a long interval from the time of Russia's departure from Afghanistan. It has now embraced even Western countries and America in its fold. These organisations are misled by Pakistan, and the situation under the Pakistani regime has only deteriorated the situation continuously. With the resumption of the Taliban rule here, this region seems to have retreated into the medieval times again. The roads are broken and schools and hospitals have been devastated.

The Afghan war against the Russian forces added a new term in the world's vocabulary, that is 'Mujahiddin'. For twenty years (from 1972 to 1992), the Mujahiddins fighting in Afghanistan have transformed themselves into unorganized but loyal Islamic fighters, who are out to re-establish Islam. In 1982, after the fall of Kabul, several partitions have been affected in Afghan Mujahiddins. Until the end of 1994, the new generation of Afghan fighters has been brought up in the Afghan refugee madrasas in Pakistan with a view to establish self-rule in Afghanistan. These people called themselves Talibs. Their social policy was fundamentalist Islamic and structure, Pashtun. For the Muslims of this area, leftism and Islam were like enemies. Due to this, it became difficult for Pakistan to aid Afghan refugees and Muhajiddins for a Mujahiddin country. In 8-9 years of the Taliban and its Mujahiddin rule in Afghanistan, the atmosphere became so suffocating that women had to keep aloof from public life. An important cause of this phenomenon was that all those educated and prosperous families fled from the country that could have emerged in public life. At one time, women used to have predominant presence in schools as teachers, but now you can see women beggars on Afghan roads. The 30-year-long civil war has destroyed the economy of Afghanistan without hope of any resurrection. Even today, it is difficult for people to live even hand to mouth. Shops are full of goods, but there are no buyers.

Farming was the main source of occupation before Islamic fundamentalism set in. About two-third population subsided on agriculture, but with damage to the irrigation structure, farming suffered huge losses. The farmers of the region earlier exported wheat, vegetables and fruits, but now they have little for their own consumption even.

According to the report of the agricultural department, Pakhtunkhwah, Swat, until 2007, contributed one-fourth of the fruit production in Pakistan, but this share has gone down to ten percent after rise of the Taliban. With its emergence has begun an era of conflict, arson, bomb explosions and blockades, which destroy as much as two-third of the total fruit produce in Swat. Farmers are not able to work in farms and gardens.

Good quality fruits were produced in the Swat region, and exported to Middle-East and Europe. The Malakand and Swat areas of the province produced abundant crops of apple, peach, apricot, plum, onion, corn, wheat and rice; however, all development has ceased to take place due to terrorism. It has become difficult even to acquire seeds, manure and pesticides for farming.

Terrorism has widely harmed fruit production in south and north Waziristan as well as Khurram, Khyber, Bajaur and Orakazai areas. The fertile land of Fata has scorched owing to lack of water, because terrorists often sever electricity connections. According to an economic survey, agriculture formed 26 per cent of the gross domestic product in 1999, which has fallen to 21 per cent in 2009. In 2000, 35 percent families were below poverty line in Fata, but now their number has risen to 66 per cent in 2011.

The Taliban rule has led to regress of the Afghans by centuries. The Taliban destroyed the Buddhist images at Bamiyan in February 2001 to destroy invaluable heritage. In the same way, the pre-Islamic artifacts of Kabul, which formed part of the national heritage, have been cast away, in a bid to destroy the historical links; and thus, the museum at Kabul has been deprived of the famous Gandhar art works and images. This is like severing one's own nose in enmity, because the world has rejected the Taliban as the source of world terrorism despite its having succeeded to occupy ninety percent of the area. In its bloody history, possibly it is the community that has witnessed the most number of widows and orphans. The worst thing to note is the fact that all those who can flee from here and who are educated, have all gone away for the protection of their lives. The history of Afghanistan reveals that its people in general and its chieftains and Ulemas of tribes in particular have completely negated the processes of modernization and democratization.

In view of the Taliban, this is *jihad*, but it came to be called Islamic terrorism. Before we further analyse the situation, it seems prudent for us to analyse the term *'jihad'*. What exactly this *'jihad'* is? How did it originate and what does it signify?

In Quran, the first explanation of *jihad* is *'Jihad al-nafas'*, which signifies 'war against one's own evils'.

If you go by the explanation of the holy text, you would wonder where from this *jihad* emerged which made bloodshed part of Islam, including the blood of innocent children; and it brought about the calamity of Islamic terrorism all over the world. How and from where did this danger emerge?

To understand it, we will have to go back into the history. As Islam progressed, like other faiths, there evolved a number of factions in it too, and with this, a new type of Islam came into being; that was political Islam. It is evident that it has fought numerous wars for power. Mohammad himself fought *'Jang-e-badar'*. If you knew about this war, you would find that it was fought to seek expansion of the faith; however, its real objective was to attain power and Islamic rule. The *Jang-e-badar* witnessed all those horrendous scenes which normally occur in any war, still the explanation given in the Quran remained unchanged.

Then in the year 1299, political Islam took a major step, which resulted into the formation of the Ottoman empire or 'Saltanat-e-Osmania'. It is a general notion that all this happened in the name of *jihad*, but it is only a fallacy, its chief cause was hunger for power.

The new definition of *jihad* was given by Mohammad Ibn-Abdul Wahab (1703-92) in the eighteenth century, by whose name Islam took a new turn, and with this emerged the deformed type of *jihad*. The faith run after the name of this Mohammad Ibn-Abdul Wahab is called Wahabi Islam, and this is the faith that wants to drown the entire world in the ocean of fire and bloodshed.

Much before the arrival of Mohammad Ibn-Abdul Wahab, the Sufi faith had come into entity which linked man with man, and which gave message of love and harmony. It rapidly expanded in Turkey, Iran, Arab and south Asia. This is quite a different thing that the Sufi faith came to be linked with a number of rituals, but it gave entirely a new form to Islam, and under it, Islam broke through its shackles of narrowness. Two significant achievements of the Sufi faith are end to slavery custom and opening doors to women's emancipation right from Ottoman to Persia and Arabia.

The followers of Maulana Rumi in Persia formed the Mevlevia faith in the thirteenth century, which opened the doors of this faith for women and gave them an equal status. It can be guessed from this fact that in the Sufi musical *Vajdana* (dance), men and women participated on equal footing. The chief pupil of Maulana Rumi was Fakhnisan. She was so influential that her tomb was constructed seven hundred years after her death by Sheikh Suleiman of the Mevlavia faith.

The great Sufi Sheikh Ibn-al-Arabi (1165-1240) was a pupil of Sufi woman Fatima Bint-e-al-Muthanna, who himself had made a cottage for his mentor, who lived there all her life and breathed her last there itself.

When Mohammad Ibn-Abdul Wahab emerged on the horizon, he destroyed the fantastic and progressive traditions one by one then developing in Islam; and he made it so narrow that there was no scope for any freedom, openness, tolerance and mutual harmony. He took up the cudgels to destroy everything that was not a part of Quran and Hadis. Until now, Islam had been divided into a number of branches. Ahmedia clan came into existence much after Abdul Wahab in the nineteenth century; while Shia, Hanfi, Mulayiki, Safai, Zafria, Bakria, Bashria, Khulfia Hambali, Zahiri, Ashri, Muntzili, Murzia, Matrudi, Ismili, Bohra and other faiths created a recognition for themselves within the scope of Islam, and these entities were recognized in Islam too.

Besides, the Sufi faith had spread all over the world, and most clans continued to link themselves with it too. However, the emergence and influence of Mohammad Ibn-Abdul Wahab resulted into an onslaught on all these clans. In his book titled *Mukhtasar Sirat-al-rasool*, he has written that any one who prays before a tomb, grave or is connected with any God other than Allah is a *mushrik* (anti-monism) and it is justified and just to shed blood of every *mushrik* and take away his property.

This was from here that the true *jihad* of Wahab was initiated, which created an army of 600 people, and their horses galloped in all directions. He started to assassinate the people of all Islamic faiths, and propagated his own ideology, and nothing else; and whoever refused to abide by him was mercilessly done to death and his property was plundered. He himself plundered the tomb of the well-known Islamic thinker Zaid-ibn-al-Khattab, and destroyed it. With this a new chapter of destruction of tombs, graves and Sufi faith started. Meanwhile, he entered into an agreement with Mohammad-ibn-Sand, who was the ruler of Diriya, and was equipped with both money and army. Both of them came together and started the use of modern weapons along with swords. They reached out to far-flung areas to impose their ideology, it became quite easy for them to destroy other faiths and beliefs. It was like a hobby for Wahab to destroy all books that might relate to other faiths. With this, he also issued a very dreaded order, that was to destroy all Sufi graves and tombs and build urinals in their place.

Today, the nation fully based on the Wahabi faith is Saudi Arabia, that has continued with the tradition of Mohammad Ibn-Abdul Wahab. This abides by this doctrine to the extent that, in 1952, it destroyed the entire graveyard where Mohammad and his entire family was buried, on the pretext that it amounted to idol-worship as people visited these graves to pray to Mohammad and his family. A part of Kaba, Almukarrama was destroyed in October 1996 for the precise reasons. Its glorious stone parts have been broken and replaced with plywood so that people could not kiss them. As according to the Wahabi sect, doing so resulted into idol-worship as per its edicts. Recently, according to a report of *The Independent*, the pillars, located behind Mecca, have been destroyed because they carried carvings of important events from Mohammad's life. One of these pillars contained a carving which annotated how Mohammad departed on *Meraj* (for rendezvous with God as per Islamic tradition).

The Wahabi sect has plundered wilfully with the entire history, beliefs, mutual harmony and marks of co-existence in Islam. It was Hitler who, in the modern times, raised the slogan of analogous identity, analogous people, analogous book and racial purity; but this type of doctrine had been propounded much earlier in Islam in the nineteenth century by the Wahabi sect.

Right from Arabia to south Asia, the Wahabi sect started to show its gore of this purity; but in the past few decades, it has made its dreaded, deformed and barbaric form even more evident. While the Mevlevia sect opened its door for women, giving them equal status, as far back as the thirteenth century, Wahabi Islam chose to enforce such cruel traditions as to burn the uncovered faces of women and stone them to death accusing them of adultery. Those who did not believe in the Wahab sect, were pronounced as non-believers and expelled from Islam, and this thing did not stop here, they went on to kill them, and justified this act as right. Such a barbarity has been meted out to the followers of Islam. You can simply imagine the calamity that might have befallen on people of other faiths, who are accused of *Kufra* as a pretext of killing them, plundering their property and kidnapping their women for forced conversion; and these things are quite common among them.

The Wahabi sect or Wahabi Islam has become a danger for the entire world. The acts of these death dealers are often called Islamic terrorism. This conspiracy is laid down in Washington and London, while executed right from Saudi Arabia to south Asia. This conspiracy is being implemented by such organisations like Al-Qaeda, Taliban, Sipah-e-Sahba, Jamat-ud-Dawa, Al-Khidmat Foundation, Jaish-e-Mohammad, Lashkar-e-Tayeba and the like, with results of bloodshed.

It was Maulana Moddi who undertook to strengthen the roots of Wahabi Islam in south Asia. The Hukumat-e-

Ilahia is part of this conspiracy, under which there is plan to root out the non-Wahabi faiths, whether within Islam or outside it, and to erect in their places a structure under which the Wahabi rule could be set up, much like Hitler had sought to do. It cannot be denied that every Wahabi step is taken in complete cognizance of America. Is America not aware that Saudi Arabia is aiding these organisations right from its soil to Pakistan and Bangladesh in every way, and its calamitous shadow has been cast on India even?

Today's Wahabi faith possesses not only swords and rifles, rather it is equipped with terrible modern weapons. It has its evil eyes on the nuclear arsenal in Pakistan too. When faith becomes insanity, it can cross all limits. The people who can raise piles of dead bodies in mosques on the day of Eid can do everything that brings sorrow to the mankind. The Wahabi sect should be referred to in this context. This danger eclipses each of that man who has stood up against this barbarity. Malala too was victimized of this barbarity.

Right from the inception of this movement in 1994, the Taliban has acted like a unified and disciplined unit. This is the reason that, after 2001, America had to conduct its most terrible military operation called 'Operation Mount Thrust' in 2006, in which a large number of people were killed in the battles between the Taliban and the Allied troops.

And after the Taliban occupied most part of Swat in December 2008, the Pakistani Government was forced to enforce the Shariat under the pressure of the Taliban.

After this, with the coming of the year 2009, the scenic Swat valley, which was once crowded with tourists, now lived under the shadow of fear and terror. Just 2,500 Taliban terrorists now have complete control over one and a half million lives. In 2011, the independent Congressional Research Service presented its report to the American parliamentarians and said that there are five types of terrorists who operate in and from Pakistan: world-centred terrorists, Afghan-centred terrorists, India-and Kashmir-centred terrorists, caste terrorists and country-centred terrorists.

Among the Afghanistan-centred terrorist groups comprise the Quetta Shura, led by Mulla Umar, an Afghan Taliban leader who operates from Quetta and Karachi. This group includes the organisation run by Jalaluddin Haqqani and his son in north Waziristan and the Hizb-e-Islami Party, led by Gulbuddin Hikmatyar operating from Bajaur tribal agency and Dir district.

The report mentions that the caste-centred terrorists are especially anti-Shiite, named as Sipah-e-Sahaba Pakistan, and the Lashkar-e-Jhangvi formed from it, and these operate mainly from Punjab. According to the report, the Lashkar is closely related with the Al-Qaeda.

According to the CRS report, the country-centred terrorists are Pashtun terrorists. These terrorists united in 2007 under the leadership of Baitulla Mehsud by the name Tehrik-e-Taliban. According to the American report, the Tehrik-e-Taliban Pakistan (TTP) was attended by a representative each from the seven Fata agencies. Later, it also included the Tehriq-e-Nafaz-e-Shariat-e-Mohammadi, led by Malulana Sufi Mohammad, which is active in north-west Malakand and Swat districts.

The report also divulged that the Haqqani network was active in north Waziristan tribal agency, which is linked with Al-Qaeda and Taliban. The TTP of Hafiz Gul Bahadur is also active in this area. This provides shelter to the Afghanistan-centred and Pakistan-centred terrorists.

Some areas on Pak-Afghan border, which provide secure shelter to terrorists include the following:

Helmand and Chagai: The Taliban had been quite active in these areas even before the 9/11 took place in America. It has its main force in Barmacha areas towards the Afghan border. Its chief commander was Mansur Dadulla. It was from here that terrorist activities have been controlled in

Nimro and Farah provinces in the west, Oregan in the north and some areas of Kandahar province in the east.

Kandahar, Quetta: Kandahar is the religious centre of Taliban activities, it was here that this rebellious organisation was founded. After the Taliban came to power in Afghanistan, its supreme leader Mulla Mohammad Umar made Kandahar his headquarter. All top leaders of the Al-Qaeda, including Osama bin Laden preferred Kandahar to Kabul. The officers of Afghanistan and Western countries have claimed that the Taliban members choose Quetta, capital of Baluchistan for shelter rather than other areas adjacent to the Kandahar border.

Zabul, Toba Kakar: The Zabul province in Afghanistan is located near Toba Kakar mountain pass which connects to Qilla Saifullah and Qilla Abdulla. The rugged terrain of this hilly area is used by the suspected Al-Qaeda terrorists under special circumstances. As there is strict watch on the border, it makes their intrusion into south Waziristan difficult. In such a case, the Taliban terrorists prefer to use the Toba Kakar pass. After their attack on south Waziristan, Pakatika Ru, the areas that the terrorists chose for their shelter importantly comprised the tribal belt of south Waziristan. The American military action in Afghanistan's Toora Bara towards the close of 2001 and in Pakatia in 2002 forced hundreds of terrorists to seek refuge in Wana here. They comprised of Arab, central Asian, Chechen, Uighur Chinese, Afghan and Pakistani terrorists. In the sub-eastern area of South Waziristan lives the Mehsud tribe, whose leader was Baitulla Mehsud.

North Waziristan, Pakatia, Khost: North Waziristan is dominated by the Wazirs. This clan also inhabits Pakatia and Khost provinces in Afghanistan. Jalaluddin Haqqani, a top Afghan terrorist, has made North Waziristan his centre of activity. He has also close contacts in the Pakistani security agencies. Haqqani has now grown old, and his son Sirajuddin has taken over the command of keeping into contact with the other terrorist commanders in the area. There is a large American military base in Khost, from where it runs its operations in Waziristan as well as targets terrorist hideouts in Pakatia and Nangarhar provinces.

Kurram, Khyber, Nangarhar: There can be no better place than Kurram to rule the roost in Afghan capital. However, the Shiite community inhabiting here is staunchly against the Taliban. This is the reason that the terrorists do not get an opportunity to settle down here. Owing to this reason, the Taliban had to struggle long to set its roots in Logar and Wardak near Kabul. Some terrorist factions in Khyber and Nangarhar keep attacking foreigners and Afghan troops; however, the Pakistani army keeps a strict vigil on them.

Mohamand, Bajaur, Kunar: As per analysts, the Bajaur tribal area of Pakistan has been the most secure hideout of Laden, Jawahiri and other top Al-Qaeda terrorists. In 1980s, Gulbuddin Hikmatyar, an Afghan guerilla leader, centred his activities round Mohmand and Bajaur. Here, different terrorist factions under the umbrella of Tehrik-e-Taliban are active in this area. They keep targeting the international troops based in Kunar province of Afghanistan.

Swat: This area, located in North Pakistan, was once ruled under the British law. It was declared unconstitutional by the court. After the Islamic laws were enforced in this district, a violent movement took place here. The rebels were brought under control, but the terrorists who arrived here from Waziristan, Bajaur and neighbouring district of Dir made their bases here after 9/11.

Swat is the only place which has come under the influence of the Taliban completely. This is owing to its topographical features too. This valley is surrounded by inaccessible mountains, and it is connected to the rest of the country by a road passing through the narrow valley, which is susceptible to blockage easily. This is the reason that the Taliban finds it somewhat easy to keep the area under its control despite its limited numbers. The Taliban is powerful in Bajaur, Khyber and Waziristan too, but it does not command its influence on the administration like it has on Swat. The border of Swat is not adjacent to Afghanistan, and it has been traditionally a peaceful area, which was often visited by tourists. There is an old history of mutual conflicts between the tribals in Bajaur, Khyber and Waziristan, but the situation had never been like this in Swat.

A strong and free Afghanistan is looked at as a threat to Pakistan's existence. Here, a moot point is: What interest has Pakistan in having a favourable government in Afghanistan? If we go through the upheaval that has been created here, we find many a factor such as strategic depth for confrontation with India, prevention of pro-India government in Kabul in order to prevent its seize by India, need for forming an Islamic centre on a wide scale right from the Arabian Sea to Caucasus mountains: all these arguments are given. If we go by the statements issued by the members of the Pakistani establishment as well as the critics there, it is clear that Pakistan wants its predominance over Afghanistan owing to these factors.

Besides the above, some imaginative factors too could be given which motivate ambition to occupy this land. If some prominent people have come to live in such a fancy world, they have to be taken seriously, because such people don't act on the basis of some illusions. Another argument that is given for this purpose is that such type of fancy, imaginative and imaginary arguments are given in order to cover up the real intentions and motives.

The actual goal of keeping Afghanistan under its control has been nursed by Pakistan out of fear for its disintegration. Until Russian occupation of Afghanistan in 1979, the real agenda of Islamabad was to check the Pakhtun and Baluch nationalists, who were supported by Kabul, from raising their voice for freedom. The Pakhtun nationalism and denial of the Durand line (it sticks to this stand even today) renders Islamabad deeply insecure, due to which it takes the Islamic doctrine as its protection as well as create political instability with a view to establish a favourable government there.

It is a historical fact that Pakistan, during the stint of Zulfikar Ali Bhutto, in 1973, started to train Islamic terrorists. This precedes much before Soviet occupation. Burhanuddin Rabbani, Gulbuddin Hikmatyar and Ahmed Shah Masud were trained in Pakistani camps; Bhutto sought to take their help to face the 'forward' policy targeted at Pakistan. Pakistan had chosen to seal its borders right from 1961. When in the beginning of 1970s, separatism started, Kabul (under the rule of Daud) supported it. Bhutto's strategy was to fight a proxy war with the help of Islamic terrorists. This remains an old method of Pakistani Government. This work was carried out under the command of Brig. Nasirulla Babar who, as the Inspector General of Frontier Corps, set up the training camps in north and south Waziristan. More than 5,000 terrorists were trained in these camps in 1973-77 period. This incident too precedes Soviet occupation. Most people assume that the Mujahideen got Pakistan patronization on as a reaction by Pakistan after Russian invasion of Afghanistan, but this is factually wrong.

Even today, the Pakistan Government fears that if Afghanistan were to have a free and strong government, as it had in 1970s, it would claim its right over Pakhtun areas of Pakistan. The people in tribal belts of Pakistan have a weak relationship with the Pakistani state; while these people have stronger bonds of age-old unity with the tribals in Khyber-Pakhtunkhwah, so-called *Bandobast* (under British management) areas. It is agreed that Afghanistan can weaken Pakistan at any hour by raising discontentment in Baluchistan; therefore, Pakistani strategists find a free and strong Afghanistan a threat to its own existence.

Of course, Pakistan cannot tell this cause as the official one, for its hollowness would surface by doing so; therefore, they hide themselves behind such fancies like strategic depth, strategic seize and central Asian opposition. Strategic depth is that valid argument which can convince patriot Pakistanis why its army is intervening in Afghanistan. If Islamabad, in support of its action, refers to India's fear in place of self-determination by Pakhtun and Baluch nationalists, its side becomes all the more justified in the international consultations. Besides, it would please the domestic and foreign Islamists unfathomably as they would then think of hoisting the green flag of Islam all along the entire border with Russia.

We can say theoretically that, if Pakistan's military-*jihadi* alliance is convinced that Afghanistan would retract from its claim of Pakhtun areas east of the Durand line, they can be kept away from destabilizing it. Therefore, there is little assumption that this would not be acceptable to Afghan nationalism.

It was not acceptable to even the Taliban rule of Mulla Omar either, so it was constituted in the hills in Pakistan on the Pak-Afghan border, and its chief objective was to oppose the America-supported government. Retired Major General Nasirulla Babar, the Internal Minister of the then Benazir Bhutto Government, set out in search of a suitable leader around April-May 1994. This process led him to Mohammad Omar Mujahid. Little is known about Omar. He remains in solitude, he seldom goes out of Kandahar, he does not talk to the media, nor does he get himself photographed. Only statements are issued in his name, so mystery revolves round him. He lost his eye in an accident. After he was chosen as the movement leader, Omar came to be called Mulla Omar in abidance with the Islamic thinking of the Taliban in order to give him authenticity. On 3 April 1996, about one thousand Ulemas elected Mulla Omar as the Amirul Mominin (highest leader of Muslims), while Burhanuddin, another leader of the Mujahiddins, was declared a criminal. Omar was presented as a khalifa (leader).

Towards the close of 1994, the basic structure had been created for the Taliban to initiate its movement. By this time, the Jamait Ulema Islam of Maulana Fazulur Rehman too was ready to gather students from madrasas. The Taliban (meaning student) was to be formed of these students. The term 'Taliban' has originated from Persian and Pushto languages, and it is the plural of the Arabic term 'Talib' which means 'one who explores knowledge'.

Following in the steps of initial khalifa, the Taliban formed the Majlis-e-Shura (the highest council), which comprised twenty members as well as 1,500 Sunni Ulemas (religious scholars) in order to give adequate representation to different castes, clans and tribes. Most of the members were Pashtuns of this Majlis led by 33-year-old Mulla Omar. Fourteen of these lost one or other body part fighting against the Soviet army. They are committed to enforce the Sharia, because the Afghan people have approved of Islam as their faith.

In 2001, when Afghanistan, the paradise of the Taliban, came under fire, the fighters headed for the neighbouring Pakistan and occupied these hills again. They might have failed to implement the severe Sharia laws in Afghanistan, but they started to work to implement the Sharia laws to rule in this new paradise called Swat.

The chief of this Taliban was Baitullah Mahsud, brother of Hakumullah, who was killed in 2009 at the age of 35 years. His younger brother, 30-year-old Hakimullah now controlled the organisation and started to undertake violent activities. It was right then when the American officials cautioned that this matter should be taken seriously, because it could mar the chances of smooth transfer of power in Afghanistan. They argued that Hakimullah might have been weakened, yet he had a large number of supporters. America announced a reward of five million dollars for any information leading to the arrest of Rehman or Hakumullah. On 1 November 2013, after the former chief Hakimullah Mahsud was killed in a drone attack, Mulla Fazlullah was appointed the new chief on 7 November 2013.

Mulla Fazlullah or Mulla Radio was basically the leader of the Tehrik-e-Nafaz-e-Shariat-e-Mohammadi (TNSSM), that aimed at implementing the Sharia law in Pakistan. Born in 1976, Fazlullah came to light in 2004 when he set up an FM radio station in Swat. This radio station was used for pouring out scathing attack on Western countries. Hardly educated, Fazlullah used to be a lift operator before. The point to note is that he increased his power by himself, and later, the Taliban and the Al-Qaeda invited him to become the area commander.

This organisation generally remained dormant until October 2005, but by this time, the earthquake that occurred in the Swat valley brought a fine opportunity for Mulla to attain power. After this calamity, Fazlullah got a great number of new cadets who sought his tutelage following disorder and starvation. He recruited this manpower on a large scale in order to expand his influence in the valley. In 2007, the action of Pakistani army on Lal Masjid provided him another chance to acquire power. This time, Fazlullah's army and Baitulla Mahsud of the Tehrik-e-Taliban Pakistan entered an alliance, which increased the power of both Baitulla Mahsud and Fazlullah.

During May to September in 2007, the temporary ceasefire in Swat provided him yet another chance, as he utilized this period to construct his political power as well as stabilize it. After October 2007, Fazlullah formed a 'parallel government' by establishing Islamic courts for enforcing the Sharia in 59 villages of the Swat valley with the help of about 4,500 terrorists.

Before we proceed further, it would be justified to know more about the Sharia.

□

2

Taliban's Sharia

It is an irony that Amir Khan Hoti, Chief Minister of Frontier Province, signed the Sharia law agreement of the Taliban. This man is none other than the great, grandson of none else but Khan Abdul Ghaffar Khan, better known as Frontier Gandhi owing to his commitment to non-violence. Amir Khan argued to justify this accord saying that he did so to prevent violence and establish peace as he had promised it to the voters during the elections.

His uncle and the chief of the Awami National Party, Afsand Yar Wali was at the target of the Taliban terrorists. He had suffered a suicide attack just three months ago, and most leaders of his party were running pillar to post to save their lives. So far as the Pakistan Peoples Party (PPP) was concerned, it was acting very carefully. President Asif Ali Zardari said that he would decide upon this matter only when it came before him for signature.

Shah Mahmood, then on tour to Washington, in order to pacify America, said that the accord was nothing but a local medication for a local ailment. The PPP neither approved of this accord, nor did it reject it. Before taking a decision formally, it wanted to see what effect it could have at least for a few months. All this while, the PPP leaders argued that there is distinction between Shariat courts and severe Islamic courts; for example, the new law will not ban women's education, nor will it impose such severe laws which are supported by the Taliban in Pakistan or Afghanistan.

On the other hand, the liberal section of Pakistan was very anguished at this accord. It opined that the government had been sold off to the terrorist elements. Iqbal Hyder, a human rights worker, termed it as 'an agreement with the devil'. He said: "How could you stand with those people who have claimed lives of hundreds of innocent people? This is a matter of principle, which should remain most important. These people must be tried for crimes against humanity."

The liberal section argued that the accord would become a predecessor for other Taliban terrorists, and they would rise to demand its implementation in other areas of the province too. Salim Khilji, a senior analyst, said: "Now I know that terrorism is the method of bringing the government to its knees." Khilji had some force in his statement, because this accord was giving the Taliban an opportunity to expand its power. The government approved this demand that it

would expand the scope of the new Shariat system in other five districts of Malakand division, in addition to Swat.

On the other hand, the Pakistani army veiled itself under the government's cover. It said that it was only following the government order by which it had been asked to keep out of the area until the next orders. If this accord brought about peace, it would relieve the army the most, because it had been suffering tragically. According to the media reports, the army had lost one hundred of its troops; while the Taliban claimed this number could be far more. Another fact remains that the Pakistani army has been trained to fight with India, and it does not find itself easy to confront with terrorism; for it does not have much experience to fight against such type of warfare, like the Indian army that has had to face such drastic situations in Kashmir, Nagaland, Mizoram and other places. Of course, the Pakistani army was to keep a watch over the developments in Swat.

A natural question that arises here is: Why did one and a half million strong population agreed to heed to those inhuman commands of the Taliban goons which are not even supported by Islam?

We can answer this question by arguing that the people were not wrong to do so. They had, in the previous elections, voted for liberal forces; but it appears that these victorious parties had no political power or willpower to protect people from the devil called Taliban.

But this leads to another question: How did the Taliban succeed to accumulate so much of power? In fact, during the period of the Riyasat or earlier rule, the justice system here was quite effective; however, after this area was blended into Pakistan, it became very corrupt; so people wanted that the Shariat courts should be set up, so that justice could be meted out quickly. Taliban took advantage of this situation and went on to expand its power. For common people, this amounted to going for an alternative that was less evil.

Now all hopes were focussed on Maulana Sufi Mohammad, Fazlullah's father-in-law. He had recently been freed after six years in jail. In 2001, he had been charged, with ten thousand Pashtuns, of fighting with the American army that invaded Afghanistan. This fight claimed the lives of 7000 Pashtuns, while he himself fled from the battle. The relatives of those killed in this battle still hate him. Effort was being made to use the same Sufi to agree to the ceasefire as proposed by the government. Fazlullah agreed for it partially, so Swat witnessed peace for some time, but no one knew how far peace could last there. Moreover, many fingers were being pointed out at the ceasefire with the Taliban.

The first pertinent question remains: Did the Pakistani Government kneel before the Talibani terrorists who wanted to take the country back to the medieval Islamic system? Or was it a well thought out strategy of the army?

Fears were being expressed, on the contrary, that this period could be used for these two factions to unite and expand their power in order to conduct raids on a large scale. Such signs emerged quite soon as the prices of weapons doubled in the area, as they were in great demand. It did not appear if this accord could be implemented as it was being explained in very many ways by different parties.

The Frontier and Islamabad governments thought that the Shariat courts were like old wine in a new bottle. On the other hand, Sufi Mohammad opined that the religious scholars would be independent judges under the accord, and their role would not be limited to only giving suggestions to the civil courts, as had been claimed by the spokesperson of Sufi Mohammad, who said that the judges would be chosen by them and they would enjoy all the powers.

Fazlullah wanted to enforce the Shariat in all areas besides judiciary. In the words of Muslim Khan, his another spokesperson: "We will run this entire area as per the book. We do not agree with any system other than ours, and if God wills, we will spread this to other areas of Pakistan soon."

It was rumoured that Sufi Mohammad would lead to establishment of peace, or would conflict with his own son-in-law. Such a scenario could benefit the army, as the army Vs. Taliban battle could turn into the one terrorist Vs. another terrorist.

Had this accord given out the message as victory to Taliban, it could have flared up terrorism in other areas of Pakistan too. If this is seen in a wider context, it could have meant a more serious situation; for in Waziristan, Pakistan-supporter Mulla Nazir, anti-government Baitulla Masud and Haji Gul Bahadur had overcome their differences to join hands. The Taliban was now expecting such Sharia courts in Bajaur too. On the other hand, in Khyber, Hamidullah had blockaded the supply line of the NATO forces. All these elements, which comprised Kashmir terrorists too, were linked to one another. The power of the demonic Taliban was expanding, and these terrorists posed a threat not only to Pakistan, but to the entire region.

And finally, the fears materialized. In 2009, Fazlullah occupied the Swat valley with his fighters, and implemented the Sharia law. He opposed even polio vaccination, and described it a Christian and Jewish conspiracy. He was against women's education too. He went round the valley in order to ask people to follow the Sharia and grow beard.

Fazlullah was the first chief commander of Pakistan Taliban who did not belong to Mahsud tribe of south Waziristan. In the Swat valley, he was known for extreme fundamentalist views. During 2008, the Taliban occupied most part of Swat. This fight had claimed more than 1,200 lives until that time, while another three and a half lakh people were forced to flee from the valley.

The rich people headed for posh areas in Peshawar or Islamabad, while the poor remained back to suffer atrocities at the hands of the Taliban; these poor pitiable people had nowhere to go.

Swat had an airport too, and it brought tourists to the valley fascinated by its scenic beauty. However, after the Taliban system came into force, the number of tourists went down drastically, causing huge financial losses to the people linked with tourism. The Taliban targeted those people in particular who served in the departments linked with law and order. They were first kidnapped and then they were rendered handicapped, sometimes went to the extent of murdering them.

Such murders were often changed into a public event to display such barbarity that could shake even the strongest, this was done to tell people how they could suffer if they chose not to obey the Taliban. The Khooni Chowk (Bloody

Square) became a symbol of terrorism. This square located in Mingora, a main town of Swat, was visited by Taliban terrorists late at night, they would hang some dead bodies with a pole in the middle; many of them were devoid of their heads. These corpses carried a note which described their name and the crime against Islam committed by them. These corpses were kept there for a definite period, just to make it clear how those, who chose to go against the Taliban orders, could suffer.

The Taliban has announced a reward of fifty million rupees each to the one who hacks off the head of the two parliamentarians from the area, and a reward of twenty million rupees each who hacks off the heads of the seven legislators from there. The residents of Swat, whose relatives are serving in Britain and America, are being targeted for a ransom of five to ten lakh rupees.

All this was happening at a place which was known as an area inhabited by the most peaceful and educated people not only in the Frontier Province, but also in the whole of Pakistan. This former estate joining Pakistan in 1969 had better schools, hospitals and police stations as compared to

other parts of Pakistan, it had an airport too, which was a point of attraction for the tourists, as they thronged here from all over the world. However, now the situation underwent a sea change; the law and order situation was completely out of control; most of the policemen fled or resigned or absented themselves from duty. The local newspapers carried such advertisements in which policemen declared that they had quit their jobs and may be forgiven for the sake of their small children. To tackle this menacing situation and to confront the Taliban terrorists, 600 local youths were chosen for special commando training; however, 450 of them disappeared during the course of training itself, while 148 of them did not report to join duty on the specified day.

Girls' education had been prohibited, causing uncertainty to education and future of more than 1,00,000 girls in the valley. In such a situation, the people of Swat were left at the mercy of these wolves who committed acts of barbarity in the name of protection of religion. People were openly beheaded and hanged; those who went against the edicts of the Taliban were shot at by veiled men wielding guns. Such incidents were also recorded on video so as to create terror among people. The population was already suffering from unemployment and starvation, and now this calamity befell them like the cruelest incidence. Eighty percent of the people of Swat earned their living by tourism, which evaporated with the rise of terrorism. There were neither workers to work in gardens, nor buyers to buy crops. People were forced to make do without basic things like fuel, food and electricity even. The only cinema hall at Mingora was closed down; television and music were banned, even the barber shops were shut down, as the Taliban pronounced that it was un-Islamic to get shaved. All these situations had the worst effect on women, children and the physically challenged.

When the Taliban chose to expand from Afghanistan to Pakistan, a bid was made to check its advance by some lively people; but Taliban is Taliban; they fancy to colour the world into the same colour. They occupied many areas of Swat; and targeted schools, especially girls' schools. They commanded to close down their schools; school buildings were razed down. It is estimated that they destroyed as many as four hundred schools between 2001 and 2009, seventy percent of these being girls'. The argument that the Taliban gave behind destruction of girls' schools was that they imparted Western education to girls. They made it hard for the girls to step out of their homes; a ban was imposed on girls' attending schools.

With the ban on girls' education, more than 1,00,000 girls of the Swat valley faced uncertainty in terms of education and future. All this was happening at a place where the ratio of women in the field of education and jobs was the highest in the whole of province. Under the new order, girls could be allowed to study only until the fourth grade, that too after their curriculum was modified. Besides, they were ordered to cover their heads with a scarf; they were banned to wear any bright coloured clothes. The women in Swat were rendered as good as prisoners within the four walls of their own houses. The central market, which once had cosmetics and bangle shops, now looked deserted and haunted, even women doctors were ordered to sit back at home; which resulted into the rise of children's death. People were dying owing to shortage of medicines and treatment.

After the Taliban rule was ended in Afghanistan, the Taliban terrorists headed for this region; not only them, a large number of American drones, Western writers, journalists and media persons too flew in, for Osama bin Laden, America's enemy number one, was yet to be killed. So the Western world now had focus on Pakistani Taliban. The American journalists and intelligentsia kept roaming about this area in Pakistan for a long time; however, with the killing of Osama bin Laden, all these people left from here in large numbers. Before leaving the Swat valley, the BBC chanced to find Malala Yousafzai who joined with those who raised their voices for the girls' rights.

The girls had stopped going to school because of the Taliban's fear. Malala's struggle begins just from this stage. She wrote a sentimental poem which was published by a newspaper in Rawalpindi. Its essence went like this: "How could the merchants of death could be the servants of faith? They have no right to be called even humans."

When the Pakistani army started its operations in May 2009, a large number of people had to flee from their homes. Malala and her family too shifted to their hometown of Shangla. With the military operations, life in Swat started to resume normalcy; however, the murder of a Pakistani journalist called Musa Khan drew attention of everybody once again. About this time, Malala too drew attention by talking about girls' rights to education. She came to the fore as Gul Makai on the BBC Urdu. The world came to know about the Taliban's rule from the view of Gul Makai.

In the year 2009, Malala wrote a diary for the BBC under her pseudonym Gul Makai, describing the evil acts of the Taliban in Swat. She started to write this diary at an innocent age of 11 years. She came to light with her diary for the BBC. She wanted to tell the world what was happening to people in her own country.

As a result of this effort, common people in the Swat region started sending their children to school in plain dress concealing their books in their shawls and sheets. The stories of her courage became a talking point that she was given the national bravery award in Pakistan. She was also named for the Children's International World Peace Award. This was how she came to be popular as an ideal girl from Swat possessing progressive views, especially for children.

It was evident that she was getting all these achievements only because she was yet an adolescent and she was bold enough to raise her voice despite her small age and living in the centre of the Taliban. She was raising her voice against vice, irreligion and injustice. When the Taliban barbarians called her name and shot at her in the school bus, the Taliban spokesperson took responsibility for the act saying that they had attacked because she was against the Taliban and was secular, so she could not be forgiven. It was clear by this admission that the Taliban was opposed to education, and it felt offended when Malala favoured education despite the ban.

The pertinent question is: Is Islam against education? Even if we accept for a moment the anti-education thinking of the Taliban, the next question arises: Could the Quran be compiled without the cooperation of educated people, the same Quran behind which they hide for their barbarous acts? Was it possible for an illiterate person to write the verses and commentaries on them? Could inventions and discoveries in medicine, engineering, or even the modern

communication system and weapons being used by the Taliban ever be achieved by an illiterate person? The same people with Talibani thinking can be seen scurrying around in search of a woman doctor when their own girls or women fall ill.

How can there be women doctors when girls don't go to school? Right from Prophet Mohammad, Hazrat Ali to all Imams and Khalifas, everybody has been seen speaking in the favour of education and educated society. Education is considered the basis of humanity, development and self-dependence. If the Taliban wishes to see the condition of an uneducated society, they don't have to go far, but they have to look at themselves. The only crime that Malala did was to lead children of common people to education, especially those who were victimized of Taliban's terror. She rose on the horizon as a lamp of light for the guardians and children wishing to have education.

And this was the reason that when the Taliban terror was diminished in Swat, Malala became a popular name in the world. She has been bestowed with a number of awards for her bravery. She has been invited as a speaker in large functions.

In the year 2009, the *New York Times* made a documentary on Malala. While shooting this documentary pertaining to Taliban's terror and ban on women's education in the Swat valley, she could not control herself and broke out crying before the camera itself. What was she getting by doing all this while she was unsure of her future? Today when she lives in Britain with her family, it is talked that her father encouraged her to achieve this glory, but will a father like to risk his daughter's life for this?

The Taliban terrorists not only threatened her with dire consequences for penning down her experiences in that phase, rather she was attacked on 9 October 2012 with a bid on her life. It was noon, about quarter past twelve, when she was returning from her school at Mingora town in the Swat valley, when the terrorists struck.

The Tehrik-e-Taliban Pakistan took over the responsibility for this attack; however, Malala was never frightened or scared or terrorized by these threats or attack; she continued boldly with her writing and spreading awareness about education.

Another pertinent question is: If the Taliban is so against the modern education, society and modern system, how does it use modern weapons and modern means of communication? In fact, any terrorist organisation including the Taliban knows it well that it can garner support only from an illiterate community and unemployed youth. On the other hand, an educated youth would have his own thinking, and would take decision as per his concepts and education. Therefore, the Taliban finds its well-being to keep the majority of people uneducated.

Committed to curtail this aspiration of the terrorists, Malala returned after her recovery, and this time, those who spoke the language of terror and violence could not do anything against her.

□

3
Malala's Family

Malala's father Ziauddin Yousafzai was the founder of his own school in the Swat valley, Kushhal Public School, as well as an educationist. Her mother, Toorpekai was a homemaker. They are now living in Birmingham with Malala and her two brothers after the attack on Malala. The Yousafzai family has its roots in an Afghan/Pathan tribe of Afghanistan called Yousafzai.

The Afghans live on both the sides of the Pakistan-Afghanistan border. As we have discussed before, the Afghan organisation is tribal, rather than political. Its chief sections include Gilzai, Mohammad, Afridi, Varjar, Karzai, Yousafzai, Mehsud and so on. There are clans and

families within the tribes. Every clan has its own chief, who represents the clan in the Zirga, or council of the elders. Every tribe is a unit in terms of geography and lineage.

At Barkana village near Shangla in the Swat valley, lived a well-known person called Rohul Amin. He had seven children, five girls and two sons, and the youngest son was named Ziauddin Yousafzai. Rohul Amin considered himself an important person and he was. Ziauddin's mother was very docile. She died before Malala was born. She often joked with her short-tempered husband that he, after her death, might be married to a woman who would never laugh.

Ziauddin stammered in childhood, so his mother was quite worried about him; he stuttered while speaking, and waited for the next word to come out of his throat. He faced much difficulty in pronouncing words with sounds beginning with *m*, *p* and *k*. Her mother was advised by someone that she should visit a *Peer* or sage who lived in a remote hill and who was known for curing this type of stammering. She travelled with him by bus for several hours and walked for one hour in order to finally reach the *Peer*. Malala's granny had her nephew with her for help. The *Peer* examined the boy and asked him to open his mouth, and as Ziauddin opened his little mouth, the *Peer* dropped his saliva into his mouth. And then he also gave her some *gur* or jaggery wet in his saliva, and asked her to give it to the child at certain intervals; he claimed that it would treat him of his stuttering, but nothing happened even after many days. Meanwhile, Ziauddin was thirteen years old now. He resolved that he would have to overcome this stammering himself, and decided to become a speaker.

One day, when he told his father that he was taking part in a public speaking competition, his father Rohul Amin was astonished, he said: "Ziau, how could you deliver a speech when you take so much of time in speaking a couple of sentences?"

Zia stammered: "That's no issue. You need not worry. Just write me my speech, I will learn it."

Rohul Amin was known for his speeches; he loved to do this. He was a teacher of theology in the nearby government high school as well as the Imam of the local mosque. He delivered sermons after the Friday prayers to listen to which people came riding horses from the mountains too. He had a large family. He had two sons, Syed Ramzan and Ziauddin. Children called him Khan Dada. Ziauddin had five sisters; and the entire family lived together in a house at Barkala village in a house having an earthen roof. Like other villages, the girls in the village kept waiting for their marriages, while boys went to school. Girls were deprived of education, rather they were even discriminated against when compared with boys. The boys were served cream, butter and milk in the morning, while girls were given tea, sometimes without milk. If eggs were served in breakfast, they would be given to only boys. When chicken was cooked, only the neck or wings were given to girls, while boys were fed better parts. Right from the time Ziauddin could see through this discrimination; which he had started hating.

There was nothing in the village that Ziauddin could do. The village was located in a narrow area in the valley, which looked more like an alley. Sometimes, he had to go to the mosque to listen to his father's sermons. Rohul Amin had studied in India, where he had seen and listened to such speakers like Mohammad Ali Jinnah, Jawaharlal Nehru, Mahatma Gandhi, Khan Abdul Ghaffar Khan and others. He had also seen how the British parted the country. At that time, he possessed an old radio which he tuned to listen to news across the world. Whenever he delivered sermons in the mosque, he would compulsorily include the news and events occurring in the country and abroad.

When Ziauddin was eight years old, the power passed into the hands of Zia-ul-Haq. Zia-ul-Haq started the process of islamisation of Pakistan and hanged the elected Prime Minister Zulfikar Ali Bhutto. Pakistan was severely criticized for this act at home and abroad. After this death penalty to Bhutto, General Zia implemented the Shariat law in the country under the command of his uncle Ghafoor, who was the head of the Jamait-e-Islami. Now, not only the civil, but also the criminal cases were dealt with according to the Shariat law. Under this law, the accused were lashed in the open and rapists were stoned to death and criminals were hanged on the squares. All this was done to pronounce that now only the Shariat law was applicable in Pakistan. All this drama ceased after Zia's departure. However, it laid the foundation of making Pakistan a fundamentalist and jihadi country.

When Ziauddin was ten years old, Russia invaded Afghanistan. This was opposed by the people of the Swat valley, because there had never been any division between Swat and Afghanistan. People on either side of the border were well-wishers for those on the other side. About this time, America armed the Taliban with dreaded weapons to confront with Russia; while Pakistan, in the capacity of being an American agent, supported the Taliban. General

Zia had never thought that aiding the Taliban could result into a devil that could destroy Pakistan itself.

For the Arab Afghans, the entire world was limited to the office of the Muslim League and Muslim Brotherhood at Peshawar, run by Abdulla Azam, a Jordanian. He was the first man who organized Islamic fighters from the world over to fight against the Russians. He was known as Mehtab-al-Kidmat. After that, Osama bin Laden, son of an Arabian billionaire, visited the *jihadi* camps. Between 1962 and 1982, 35,000 *jihadists* from 43 Islamic countries fought with the Mujahiddins in Afghanistan against Russia. This camp became the base for future Islamic extremists. Writing about this war, Samuel Huntington has written that the goal of these Islamic organisations was to enhance the dominance of Islamic organisations over the non-Islamic troops. It left behind a heritage of the experienced Islamic fundamentalists.

It was at this stage that Osama bin Laden visited Afghanistan and started funding for *jihad*. These Arabic fighters followed the Wahabi sect, and they fought a number of battles shoulder-to-shoulder with the Taliban; they played a vital role in mass massacres, especially those of Shiites. After this, Kabul was occupied by the Taliban. However, the ISI of Pakistan was unnerved when the Taliban refused to accept the Durand line. It was further disappointed when the Taliban refused to retract Afghanistan's claim over the North West Frontier Province.

The tribal groups in the tribal belt, administered by the Frontier Province, had completely become fundamentalist. A wave of terror was felt in Pakistan when some leaders, greatly influenced by the Taliban, demanded to impose the Sharia law in Swat, then known as a 'holiday spot'. The Sharia law was enforced in Swat for some time too, but Pakistan had to send its forces to take Swat back from the fundamentalists, paying a high cost in the process. Today,

all Talibani fighters are engaged in destroying none else but Pakistan, much like Bhasmasur of Hindu mythology. On seeing whatever is happening in Pakistan, we cannot overlook the fact that it was General Zia who, under the Operation Zibralter had planned to annex Afghanistan's Pakhtunistan. He attempted to do this in order to make up the loss of land that it lost in the form of Bangladesh. Not only this, he had planned to annex Indian Kashmir under the Operation Topak. General Zia did not succeed in carrying out these intentions, but the Afghans could realize that his intentions were not right. Now there is a section of Afghanistan Taliban, functioning in Pakistan adjoining the borders, which is anxious to annex a part of Pakistan into Afghanistan by force.

During those days there were no proper educational facilities like school buildings or electricity. Most schools were held in the open, under the broad blue sky. Students were discriminated against in schools too.

The teachers paid more attention to pretty students with white skins. While Ziauddin was dark and short, his mother took special pain to look after him. Ziauddin tried to copy his father's good handwriting skills but Amin never said a word of appreciation. During his school days, he had to be contented with the old books as his father brought him old books from his students.

Rohul Amin was considered a miserly person, yet he sent Ziauddin in the government high school for modern education. He was criticized by the Imams. He wanted his son to become a doctor but Ziauddin was weak in mathematics and science, so there was every doubt about his success in this field.

Rather, Ziauddin took part in the district public speaking competition. Rohul Amin acceded to his request for a speech after much convincingness. It was a fine speech, and Ziauddin prepared well, and went on to obtain the first place in the competition. When he climbed up the stage to receive the first prize, he found his father among the audience clapping and cheering him. It was for the first time that he had admired his son. After this, Ziauddin never looked back in his life.

All this while, Ziauddin got a chance to seek admission in the Jehanjeb College, considered to be the best college in Swat. However, Rohul Amin refused to bear the expenses. Amin had studied in Delhi where no fee was paid. He lived in a mosque then where free food was served. He studied there as a *Talib* or student. Of course, there was no fee in the Jehanjeb College too, but it needed a large living expenditure. Those days there was no provision for an education loan, and there was no one from the family there with whom he could stay during the course of his education. Now, the tough problem before Ziauddin was that he could not have got higher education without stepping out of the village. By this time, Ziauddin's mother had died, else she might have stood by his side. Ziauddin requested many of his relatives. Finally a relative named Nasir Pacha got ready to help him. When Ziauddin entered college, General

Zia-ul-Haq had died in a plane crash. Ziauddin started to work in the student union. He became a good speaker and debater in the college; therefore, he was elected as the general secretary of the Pakhtun Student Federation. Gradually, he set on the path of completing his education and pay attention to his living.

Ziauddin was good at studies right since the beginning, and he was staying at Karsat for his education. Here also lived Jansher Khan, whose daughter was Toorpekai. She had just crossed the threshold of adolescence, while Ziauddin lived just in neighbourhood. They saw each other and it was love at first sight. It led to some conflict, but the ultimate outcome was their wedding.

Toorpekai was one of the seven siblings. Her father Jansher Khan was engaged in local politics and did not pay much attention to his children. Toor attended school right since the small age. She was the only girl in the class, though none of her cousins went to school. One day, she had something else going in her mind. She sold off all her books and ate up sweets from the money she got in lieu of them, and ever since, she never turned towards any school.

Toor loved Ziauddin, but she regretted her act of selling books because here was a man in her life who had read a large number of books; who wrote poetry and speeches, and who had a dream to open a school. On the other hand, Toor never knew how to read and write. In such a situation, she could not have helped him in realizing his dreams in any way.

When Ziauddin completed his college education, he joined a private school as the English teacher, but the salary was as little as Rs. 1600, not enough to meet both ends for himself, leave alone to fulfil the demand of money that his father wanted from him. Of course, he saved a little amount despite the low salary as he aspired to marry to Toorpekai. He had a friend, Mohammad Naim Khan, who was a teacher in the same school. Both of them were unhappy with the school administration. In a controversy with the school administration, Naim lost his job.

Ziauddin and Naim possessed similar views; so they decided to open a school of their own. They chose to open it at Shahpur village, as it was a large one while there were many other schools in the vicinity.

When they arrived at Shahpur, they saw that there were banners about some other school. Therefore, they decided to open an English medium school at Mingora. Their thinking behind this was that Swat was a tourist place and people would take interest to learn English.

Ziauddin had not yet resigned from his job; so, Naim went round Mingora for a building on rent. One day, he informed Ziauddin that the building had been located, he could visit and inspect it, so that they could finalise their plan. This spot was near a river in a posh colony. It was a two-storey building, in the lower part of which a school was already running; however, the school owner had opened a hotel in Turkey, so he was vacating it now.

When Ziauddin saw that place, his joy knew no bounds. It seemed as if his dream was going to be realized soon.

Not very long after, the school was started, and both of them set out to look for children for admission, but they did not get many children. The upper portion of the building had provision for their living. They faced a problem when a lot of Ziauddin's guests started to visit, the worse was that these guests stayed there over many days. Ziauddin and Naim invested their capital of Rs. 60,000 in the school, and they had also taken a loan of Rs. 30,000. With the visit of guests, their living bill rose. Naim little liked being host to so many guests. He often explained to Ziauddin that they were old friends, but then they were business partners too, so they must not involve themselves in extravaganza. Naim proposed to the extent that he would have to pay a fine whose guests visited. This led to a deadlock between the two, compelling Ziauddin to think to open an independent school of his own. He wanted to separate from Naim, but he was facing the shortage of money.

It was at this junction that Hidayatulla, Ziauddin's old friend came forward, and he wished to become a partner in Naim's place. This was how Naim's partnership was terminated and Hidayatulla became the new partner. The school was named Khushhal Public School.

Ever since Ziauddin did not look back. The number of students in the school was small in the beginning, but its name spread with time. Meanwhile, Ziauddin married Toor, and they now lived at Mingora. Later, Hidayatulla too separated to open an independent school, but they told people that it was another branch of the same school.

All days are not alike. When Toorpekai grew expectant for the first time, Ziauddin did not have enough money to

admit her in any of the hospitals for delivery. Therefore, he sought the services of a nurse, and it was how a daughter was born. The Pashtuns in Swat think that the birth of daughters is sorrowful and unlucky for the family. Therefore, nobody visited the family to congratulate them on the birth, except one, that was Jehansher Khan, who also brought some money in addition to gifts. He had also brought a booklet which enumerated the lineage of the family. This booklet carried the names of male members from the time of Ziauddin's great-grandfather, but it avoided the names of girls altogether. Ziauddin possessed a different type of thinking right since the beginning. He felt perturbed on seeing this discrimination, and drawing a line in the family tree under his name, he wrote the name of his newly born daughter, Malala. Yes, Ziauddin Yousafzai named his daughter after the name of the Pashto poetess Malalai, who had fought bravely in the second British-Afghan battle in 1880 at Mevand and defeated the enemy. She had sacrificed herself at the small age of 18 years. Malalai was a Pashtun woman hailing from Mevand, located near Kandahar. The Mevand battle (27 July 1880) is remembered in history because it was Malalai who motivated the Pashtuns for the battle when they were pitched against the British. This battle was fought at a time when Malalai was already betrothed. Her fiancé and father too joined the battle. She joined the battlefield in order to nurse the wounded. When the British seemed to overcome the Pashtuns, Malalai started singing poetry in her dialect and motivated her people. When the British killed the Pashtun fighter holding the flag, Malalai took up the flag herself and joined the battlefield as a combatant. She was killed in it, ever since the name Malalai became a popular name.

Ironically, the word Malala in Pashto signifies 'sorrowful', but Ziauddin overlooked this meaning, and brought before his eyes the image of Malalai, and he named his daughter as Malala after the great woman-warrior.

Jehansher Khan laughed at this name, he joked about his misunderstanding, but Ziauddin remained unmoved; he had come to love his fairy-like daughter, fair-like pearl with big dark eyes; he loved her more than the entire world.

Malala's grandfather expressed displeasure over such a name for the girl, but Ziauddin did not back off. It has already been mentioned that he lacked funds.

When Malala was two years old, her brother Khushhal was born. He was very weak at birth, his father considered him like a reed, and was afraid that he might be blown away with the wind. However, he remained an apple of Toorpekai's eyes. On the occasion of his birth, Toorpekai asked for a new crib, but Ziauddin declined describing it as an expensive demand. He asked when Malala could be brought up in the old crib, what the problem with Khushhal was. A few days later, yet another son was born named Atal. Ziauddin was satisfied that his family was now complete. This cannot be denied that this family was still very small if you keep the area in the mind, as normally people had seven to ten children here.

This was how Malala had a limited family, her parents, two brothers, and of course a few hens; and within this scope was limited her life. She was born in a community where daughters were not respected. When she was born, some relatives visited and said to her mother, "You need not worry, you will have a son next time." However, her father was very affectionate towards her. He said that her daughter had something unique in her since her childhood, which drew him to her.

The most important thing for Ziauddin, the owner of Khushhal Public School, was to teach children. He had been working among his people for a long time, and he wished that the life in the Swat valley should improve, he wanted democracy to prevail in his country. This dream of his did not materialize, rather there came Taliban terrorists; and with this, the people of Swat started to lose the few rights they had. It was not possible for him to accept all this. His conscience called him: "What are you waiting for? Whom are you waiting for?"

Ziauddin could see that even the government officials were forced to quit from the valley. The Taliban forced their elders to leave the area. They started to hunt even policemen. They had even Ziauddin in the list of their targets, he was threatened a number of times, but he and several of his friends chose the path which could free their land from the scourge and bondage of the Taliban. When Malala joined this battle, he was happy that she had joined him to raise the voice in the favour of education and basic human rights. According to him, those government departments should feel guilty who could not protect their land, their people and children. He felt happy that he was able to do something in his life.

In the year 2000, Masud, a Tajiq leader, was emerging as a nationalist leader of Pakistan. In September 2001, the Al-Qaeda attacked him in wile. They sent two Tunisian terrorists in the garb of photographers-journalists for an interview with Masud. Overlooking the warning given to him, Masud got ready for the interview. Dressed as journalists, these two assailants set the camera, and when Masud sat in front, one of them clicked it causing a massive explosion at his face, which wounded him badly, later he succumbed to his injuries. These two assailants were apprehended and shot dead, but the harm had already been done. The murder had been planned and executed in a very tricky way. This murder was discussed the world over, and the increasing might of the Taliban could be guessed. Ziauddin too could perceive the advancing steps of the Taliban terrorists.

In fact, in January 1995, the extremist Taliban fighters surrounded capital Kabul, and by 1996, the whole of Afghanistan fell under their rule. Ahmed Shah Masud rejected the extremist ideology of the Taliban, and took up

arms against it. He became the leader of the Joint Islamic Front, which was also known as the Northern Alliance. Just two days after his death, terrorist attacks were carried out in the United States on 11 September 2001, better known as 9/11; it was after this that America and its allies entered into as agreement with Masud's front and overthrew the Taliban from power. However, the Taliban continued to execute its unholy and sacrilegious intentions. By 2007, this advance became massive and threatening, which started to have negative impact on the private lives of people too. Due to this, Ziauddin started to oppose all this in a low tone.

Malala was greatly influenced by her mother since the beginning, as it was she who motivated Ziauddin and Malala. When the family faced difficult times in Swat, it was Toorpekai who stood by them saying that they were doing the right thing; because truth was with them, and that God was with them, so they must not backtrack. Toorpekai had never been to school herself, but now she was studying at home; she often sought Malala's help in studies. This aspiration to learn the unknown also enthused Malala to continue with her study. Toorpekai often told her sons that she could not study, which she always regretted; she must have gone to school when it was the right time for her. She convinced the boys to study because it was the right time for them, else they would have to regret later.

When Malala grew a little, she joined school. She would get up early in the morning. Looking at her aptitude, Ziauddin would carry her along and made her sit in the classroom, where she sat joyfully. In the beginning, she said that she wanted to be a doctor, as she had seen the girls around her become doctors or teachers after education. However, when she found that there were able doctors in the country to look after health needs of the people, but the country lacked an able leader who could solve their other problems, she decided to become a leader in order to treat the ills eating the country.

The family members had no objection to her education. She went to school with their concurrence, while there were many other girls who were not sent to school by their parents. If she saw a girl of her age not going to school, she would tell her to accompany her. In the beginning, it was considered no major issue, but people thought after some time that it was not the right thing for her to do so; so they complained at her house. Her parents told her not to do so.

Malala was yet a child, but she could understand well the world's ways. She could understand the distinction between a boy and a girl. Storms of questions rose within her. She asked herself why other girls could not go to school when she could. She asked this question at school. Her father was an educationist, so this wish of hers was communicated to her family. She was told that her family was liberal, but such was not the case with others so they were not being sent to school. As Malala was not wrong either, her parents never rebuked her for this.

Malala played with her brother Khushhal as he was two years younger than her, though Atal was much younger.

She never liked when he teased her, told her all the things, and this led to a quarrel between the two. She always liked democracy, but on such occasions, she felt that dictatorship was not that bad if her brother was to be shut up. She always favoured equality and human rights. She supported the freedom of speech but when her brother teased her, she would set out to teach him a lesson. She would run after him, who then would hide behind his mother's shield; and then Malala would go to her father. Ziauddin would take her up in his lap and ask, "Yes, baby, what's the matter?" He would laugh at the childish quarrel and childlike innocence.

Ziauddin always felt something unique in her; for, she discussed with her father politics for long after the two boys were fast asleep.

As they lived in a small house, they had to eat food sitting on the floor after a mat was spread. There was a girl of her age in the neighbourhood, called Safina; whose family too had two boys named Babar and Basit. They all would play cricket in the street. In the evening, when Ziauddin was free, he would tell the children tales of their Pashtun forefathers, warriors and rulers. It was from her father that Malala came to know that she belonged to a tribe called Yousafzai. She was fond of listening to the tales of this tribe.

Malala loved to go to school like other children of her age, but she did not know why she should go to school. As the prohibitions were intensified in the valley, so did she grow up, and now she could know the significance of education. The Taliban had not yet imposed a ban on girls' education in the valley, yet rumours were ripe there that the Taliban would issue different types of *firmans* to prohibit girls from going to school. Malala heard all these things, and with this, she strengthened her opposition against the Taliban's unreasonable stand. She felt that education was a great gift, only the Taliban was out to ban it, so she was determined to get it anyhow.

□

4
Malala's Resistance

Malala was eleven years old when the Taliban started to oppose the running of schools in the Swat valley. The Pakistani Government appeared to have lost its control over the valley. The Taliban commander had set up his own radio station illegally, which relayed programmes morning and evening for two hours. This broadcast mainly centred round propaganda of Islamic teachings. As there were not many television sets in the valley, people used radio sets to listen to news and music. This radio was called Mulla Radio. It kept parroting Islamic teachings all the time, how one should live in Islam, how prayers should be offered, how to remain clean, and the like. This was the reason that people, especially women, listened to this radio with interest. When the Taliban came to know that people were much influenced by their propaganda, they started to execute their real agenda.

They started to destroy the schools which imparted progressive education, and kidnap children going to school. Girls were forbidden to watch television. They closed down girls' schools. They prohibited right from playing music in the car to playing on the road. They mostly stressed their opposition to girls' education. This had profound effect on the people in the valley. Scared of this attitude of the Taliban, they started to stop their children from going to school. Even in this small age, Malala could guess that it was inevitable to be educated in order to enable man to lead a successful and happy life and fill him with self-confidence. Malala was in the seventh grade when the school was closed down following the Taliban's order. Until this time, she did not yet know even ABC of politics, what she knew abundantly clearly was that she and her friends loved to go to school, and maybe they would no more be able to go to school any more.

Such situations help children to grow up rather before time. Malala too was thinking in a more mature way than the girls of her age. She, like other girls, was badly hurt because of this prohibition. She now well understood that the media is a powerful means to convey one's views, so she wanted to find some way to convey her idea to the Taliban. She wanted to tell them about their wrong acts which Talibani's were doing in the name of religion.

As such, she wrote a very sentimental poem in Urdu, under the guidance of her father, discussing this state, which was published by a newspaper in Rawalpindi too.

She condemned the Taliban in this poem. She asked how the merchants of death could be servants of religion; they even lacked the right to be called humans. Her voice reached the Taliban, but it had rather an adverse impact. They considered her a disobedient girl and started to hate her.

And then, Malala came to know about Anne Frank. Born on 12 June 1929, Anne Frank belonged to Frankfurt in Germany. In 1933, when she was just four years old, her parents were forced to quit Germany. They took her to Amsterdam in the Netherlands, but they were trapped there too as the Nazis occupied that territory in 1940. The Nazis inflicted atrocities on the Jews there too, and in July 1942, this family had to seek refuge in her father's office building to save their lives. About two years later, they were subjected to a foul game, and were arrested. Like other Jews, they too were sent to concentration camps. Seven months later, Anne died of typhoid in the camp, her sister had died just a week ago.

Now, the family was survived by only Anne's father, who returned to Amsterdam at the end of the war. There he found Anne's diary, in which she had written about her life in hiding. After many efforts, he succeeded to get this diary published in 1947. It was later translated into English, and it was then published in 1952 titled *The Diary of a Young Girl*.

Anne was gifted this diary on the occasion of her thirteenth birthday. She described her life in it from 12 June, 1942 to 1 August 1944. Later, this diary was translated into as many as 67 languages, and this became a top-selling book in the world. This also formed the basis of a number of dramas and films. Anne is known for the quality of her writing as well as the most well-known and talked-about victims of the holocaust. She was one of those one million Jew children who had to lose their childhoods, families and lives.

Years later, people came to know about the lives of people from the viewpoint of a girl. Malala too wanted to do something of the sort; she wanted to tell the world what was in her mind.

Malala says: "Maybe this was the day when I realized the importance of education. I never knew why I went to school earlier. Now, the doors to school were closed down, but the doors to books opened up."

With these views, Malala came out in the open to propagate education and oppose the Taliban's anti-education stance. She also started to speak in the favour of education, progressiveness, liberalism and secularism.

Her fearlessness was brought out by the bureau chief of Don Television News of Peshawar, who used the electronic media for this purpose. It was by chance that the bureau chief was at the Khushhal Public School in Mingora circa November 2007. On the way, he saw the Talibani fighters dragging out drivers out of the cars in order to check if they carried anything that disrespected the Shariat law such as DVD, wine or the like. He saw the two-storey Khushhal Public School at a little distance from the market. The school carried the maxim of the school in Arabic: *Oh my Lord, give me more learning*. He gave a thought to this maxim if, under the Taliban rule, the girls studying there obtained such learning or not. Thinking so, he walked to this school.

The bureau chief met the girls studying in the fourth grade of that school and asked if any of them would like to give an interview on television about their views on Taliban terrorism and destruction of schools. Contrary to his anticipation, numerous hands went up into the air.

The bureau chief was stunned to see this, because it was no ordinary thing for girls to come before the public or speak publicly. His astonishment was not unreasonable either. He found it difficult to decide which girl to choose for the interview, but then other girls and the school principal solved his problem. The same evening, a television interview by a little girl with brown eyes became the talking point. This girl was none other than Malala.

Ziauddin Yousafzai knew it well that it was no ordinary thing for him to allow his little daughter to go on the national channel, as he came from a fundamentalist rustic community of Pakistan that was not ready to modify its customs and traditions like those of the elite classes living in Karachi or Lahore. With her coming on the television screen, Malala became a star for her schoolmates and neighbourhood. Of course, it did not matter much to her. In her small age, she had come to know how to live in an atmosphere where violence was the order of the day. She had seen numerous wounded and dead people. With this, she made her father's resolve an aim of her life by which they wanted to bring about change in the Swat valley.

With the changing situation, she got an opportunity to write a diary for the BBC with her father's inspiration. She wanted to write the diary in her own name. She did not want to use a pseudonym in order to conceal her identity; but for security reasons, she chose Gul Makai (literally a 'corn flower'). She was given this name by Abdul Hoi Kakkad, former reporter of BBC Urdu service. He used to take her dictation on telephone. According to Abdul Hoi, Malala was obviously a very intelligent and smart girl.

He recalled his meeting with Ziauddin and said that it was by chance that he happened to meet Malala through her father. It happened during December 2008 when the Taliban imposed prohibition on girls' education in the north-western Swat valley. The year changed from 2007 to 2009, and now Malala was in the seventh grade.

Abdul Hoi had been sent to cover a story for the Urdu service of the BBC. He was assigned to motivate a young student – boy or girl – to write a blog for the BBC's popular site. The simple concept behind this was to bring forth the life of people under the Taliban from the viewpoint of a school student. The BBC editors were looking for a student who could write about the prevailing situation there.

Abdul came to know about Ziauddin through his contacts and editors. He found out about him that he was running a private school in Swat and was an outspoken member of the anti-Taliban Qaumi Zirga (or community legislative council). At that time, he was busy drawing others' attention towards the pitiable condition of his motherland.

Ziauddin took him to girls of the tenth grade who were curious to write the blog, but they backed off under the pressure from their parents. At this, Abdul stressed upon Ziauddin for their replacement. Finally, Ziauddin's own eleven-year-old daughter happily agreed to accept this challenge. Recalling that moment, Ziauddin says that many girls of my school wanted to write the blog, but they backtracked owing to their parents' pressure. I could only pressurize my daughter, so I did not force her to come before the media, but she was the only one whom I could help to get the blog written on my own responsibility.

Swat was passing through the worst period at this time. The Taliban had been fighting on the remote western tribal areas along the Afghanistan border, and now it was expanding its reach; and now it had succeeded to occupy a strategic district, and brought it under its autocratic rule.

The place was experiencing thefts, robberies, arsons, suicide attacks and targeted killings regularly. Raising one's voice against the Taliban in Swat was practically as good as signing one's death warrant.

Abdul Hoi was greatly influenced by Malala's intelligence. As Swat suffered from long electricity cuts and lack of Internet service, Abdul was forced to take her dictation on telephone.

Abdul wished to protect Malala's identity too, so he used the cellphone of his wife for conversing with her, as his own telephone was under surveillance by Pakistan's detective agencies, because he had been reporting the Pakistani military campaign against the Taliban. As a security measure, he gave her a pen name Gul Makai, which in Pashto meant a corn flower.

Malala was a little hesitant in the beginning, but she gained her confidence with the passage of time; she felt quite easy with her work. She soon understood that her blogs should comprise the activities of the Taliban along with those of the Pakistani army and people of Swat. He started to dictate Abdul on daily basis. Her blog attracted a large number of people in Pakistan too, and when the BBC undertook translation of her blog for the world's viewers, she gained international recognition. Everybody was now talking about Gul Makai. When some people discussed Gul Makai with Ziauddin, he could not say that she was none else but his own daughter. As expected, the Taliban was not at all happy with her fame.

Her world fame brought people's attention to the local issues which she had raised in her blog; but her parents continued to nourish and groom an independent personality of their eldest child who was courageous and straight forward.

Ziauddin, who dressed his short hair very well, continued be an inspiration behind Malala. Once, he said to Abdul: "I encouraged Malala right from her small age to groom into an independent personality. I think she is my friend, my comrade, she can march with me, she can trust my mission and my views with closed eyes. I would not like to clip my daughter's wings, who wants to fly high in the sky."

Ziauddin was standing erect in opposition to the Taliban terrorists, who had changed Swat into a private estate of Maulana Fazlullah by 2005.

Ziauddin was one of those few local workers who had courage enough to speak against the Taliban openly. He was appreciated for his humourous and sharp speeches; his talks were often quoted in tea houses and drawing rooms widely. The sole objective of his effort was to unite people against Taliban's atrocities.

He spoke in an assembly: "Swat has been taken as a poultry farm, where the Taliban keeps murdering us one by one. We should respond to this injustice collectively. It is better to raise our voices than to surrender ourselves in their slaughter house."

During 2008, when the Taliban's terror ruled supreme, the terrorists identified Ziauddin as one of the opponents of the FM radio broadcasts, and decided to punish him with death; however, Ziauddin did not waver. He remained underground for several months rather than abandon his struggle publicly. Those days, he never stayed at any place for the second night in tandem.

After a large military operation was undertaken in 2009 to expel the Taliban out of Swat, it was like a black period because the Taliban still persisted. During this period, Malala and her mother always had a ladder along the wall in the house, so that it could prove to be the last lifeline for Ziauddin if he had to flee on the entry of the Taliban terrorists in the house. Amidst the terrible atmosphere of dread and threat, many of his friends and relatives urged him to retract his open opposition to the Taliban. However,

Ziauddin never expressed regret about his opposition against the extremists, rather he said: "The cowardly always hope that you are terrorized, while the brave expect you to stand boldly." He argues that the factor behind the failure of the Pakistani military regime is the fact that the security establishment of the country itself has used the Taliban comrades against India and Afghanistan while it remained behind the curtain. He opined that the people were first misled to become the Taliban terrorists, and then they were held responsible for being extremists, and then identified them as the Taliban. When people were killed in Taliban violence, the government offered to pay a small relief too, which is more like a cruel joke.

In his speeches, Ziauddin compared the people of Swat with cattle, and described their life as still cheaper than that of a cattle. He said: "The relief given for the loss of life of a Pashtun is less than the cost of a buffalo."At that time, the government paid merely one thousand rupees as the relief for a civilian's death caused by the Taliban, while the cost of a milch animal in Pakistan was as much as three thousand rupees. Criticizing severely the government, he said: "A state ought to treat its citizens like its children, but unfortunately, our parents have deceived us."

If the daughter of such a bold spokesperson brought out the misdeeds of the Taliban before the world, it could be no strange thing.

In her diary, Malala kept writing about the misdeeds of the Taliban in the Swat valley. She wrote how the girls of her age considered these Taliban terrorists worse than even the devils, while these people were foolish enough to consider themselves as messengers of God. Meanwhile, the heartrending programmes, being relayed by the popular BBC Urdu Service by Malala started to become very popular in the Swat valley as well as the whole of Pakistan and Afghanistan. She went on to describe the actual situation prevailing in the Swat valley. She would also describe the negative impact of the Taliban terror and its atrocities being inflicted on the people. At the same time, she would emphasise on spread of education. It was through her diary that Malala not only created awareness among the people of the region, but also raised them against the Taliban.

A few months before she came under the bullet fire, Malala wrote in her diary: "They are aware that they have deprived the people of education in the name of Islam; they feel threatened that a small girl could divulge their reality. Now, the girls are no more afraid of guns. They go to school, they now understand that there is a deep conspiracy to keep the women uncivilized in the name of Sharia law. They are proving themselves courageous; they are playing a significant role for this task. She could be shot dead any day by the Taliban, or she could come under an acid attack on the face. But we have to overcome these threats, so I would keep fighting for self-respect of the Swat valley until my last breath."

This diary started to grow so popular that the Taliban found itself bewildered by its remarks. Its spokesmen claimed a number of times that they had investigated that there was no girl named Gul Makai in the whole of the Swat valley; nobody could have dared to do so in view of their power.

Now, Gul Makai was a point of discussion in the valley owing to her blog. She published her diary for the BBC for ten weeks. When Malala and her family left the Swat valley before the military operation began in 2009, this diary was stopped, and with this, her association with the BBC too came to an end.

This was the time of January 2009. She had started writing it initially describing her fear following the terrible dream that she had on the night of a Saturday in 2009.

It was the day of Saturday in the year 2009 – a Saturday of the onset of winters in the new year. This night Malala saw a very dreadful dream, in which she saw military helicopters and Taliban fighters. She had been seeing such dreams after the military operation began in the Swat valley. Troubled by these dreams, when she rose early, she had her breakfast to get ready for school. Just then, she came to know that the Taliban had pronounced that no girl must go to school from 15 January. This shook her inside. Despite this prohibition, she got ready and left for school. She was feeling scared of going to school.

That day, only 11 out of a total of twenty-seven girls were present in the class. This number diminished because the people felt scared to send their girls to school after the Taliban's prohibition. At this time, she also came to know that three of her friends had quit school to go to other places with their families, like Peshawar, Lahore and Rawalpindi. This was a very bad time for Malala and her friends. They were just talking on this issue, when the school was over. All of them started to walk home with a lot of questions raining down on their minds. They were unsure what would happen the following day. She started to walk back home with a heavy heart, and just about this time, she heard a heavy voice on the way, that shouted: "I will not leave you."

Malala was already scared, so she was out of her wits fully when she heard this voice, she now started to walk quicker. A little distance away, she looked back, and she found that a man walked behind her talking on phone and threatening somebody with dire consequences. She heaved a great sigh of relief at this, her face regained its lustre with a light smile. When you are scared, you could take even a rope for a snake. That day, Malala thought that she would go to a boarding school if her education came to a stop there. But all other girls could not go to boarding school, could they? She thought, and she thought deeply. It would amount to being selfish if she went to a boarding school. Then she thought that she would study at home, and would open a school secretly, where other girls would join her. But she knew this possibility could not materialize into reality. She decided that she would continue to go to school in garb, and if somebody asked her which grade she studied, she would mention a smaller grade, because the Taliban had not yet imposed prohibition on small classes for girls. She kept thinking numerous things around this topic.

Generally, Malala rose a little late on Sundays, but the situation had taken such an ugly turn that she did not like anything, she was often disturbed from sleep due to the bomb explosions that occurred in the middle of the night. So, she rose early, and her father gave her a piece of terrible news.

That day, three corpses had been recovered from the Green Chowk. It was evident that it was the act of the Taliban terrorists. Malala felt bad about this the whole day. She could remember those Sundays when the military operation had not yet begun, she used to go for a picnic in different places on Sundays, like Mir Gujar, Fiza-e-Ghat and Kanju and other places. She rued that they had not gone for a picnic for one year and a half. She, like other common children, loved to wander about, play and bathe in the natural springs and falls, but it was a crime in the opinion of the Taliban. Earlier, she went out for a walk after the night meals, but after the situation deteriorated, they returned home in the evening itself.

Malala noticed that people kept on working in their houses as they used to do before, but now she found that people were not enthusiastic, joyful and gleeful. They all worked as if they were living and breathing machines. As this thought dawned on her, she remembered that she could no more wear the school uniform, as her headmistress had asked the girls to wear homely clothes to school. Malala could have jumped in joy had this command been given under normal circumstances, but this command had been given in order to protect girls from the Taliban, so she grew sad and hopeless. The family members repeatedly advised all girls to carry their books and notebooks hiding under their shawls. Malala wont to oppose all this. She could not tolerate all these bans but she was forced to abide by all these instructions for the sake of her own security.

Malala went to school wearing her favourite pink dress. She noticed that all other girls wore ordinary clothes which made the school feel like a home. Any girl could have felt happy at this, but Malala felt that all other girls were thinking if their school was under the Taliban's threat. Will all of them be killed? Just about this time, a friend approached Malala and asked in the name of the Quran if the school could be attacked by the Taliban. The assembly bell went off before she could say anything in response. They walked to the assembly hurriedly. That day again, the girls were asked not to wear bright and colourful clothes, as the Taliban could be wary of them. Every girl was scared now. Malala too felt scared, but she did not divulge this to anybody. She did not allow her fright to overcome her thinking; she felt that she must get education somehow. She did not allow the terror to surface in her mind which could check her from getting education.

Every girl, including Malala, thought why the Taliban wanted to control their education, their dress and lifestyle. What will they get from all this mess?

In this terrifying atmosphere, Malala and her friends were happy to watch a piece of good news that the curfew had been lifted off Shikrada in the Swat valley after fifteen days. Their English teacher belonged to this area, and it could be possible that he would join school once again. They all felt happy at this, but they were also anxious about his safety. Even if their education resumed, they were unsure how long it could continue.

Ziauddin Yousafzai could notice the changing circumstances well. He felt that all these circumstances had profound impact on Malala, so he decided to take the entire family to district Bunir to spend their holidays on account of Muharram Al-haram. Malala loved Bunir greatly. Surrounded by hills on all sides, the green valley looked still more glorious than Swat. Swat lacked peace and tranquility, but these were abundant at Bunir. There was no sound of gunfire, there was no terror in the atmosphere; Malala and her family were immensely joyful there.

There is a tomb of a Peer Baba at Bunir, which is thronged by people. Ziauddin saw that a lot of people visited the tomb to seek wishes. In the fair, he asked Malala to buy bangles, earrings, lockets and the like, but she did not like anything; as it is, she was little interested in cosmetics or jewellery.

Malala came to know about an interesting aspect of Bunir from Ziauddin. This was related to the game of archery. An acquaintance had told him had Robin Hood been born in Khyber Pakhtunwah of Pakistan, he too could have played with crossbow and arrow much like the people there.

They were amazed to find that archery was being played in the region for thousands of years and is known as *Mokha* in the local dialect. It would not be false to say that it was an important part of the culture there. The crossbow used for archery was made from deer horn, called *Darveshi Gulel* in the local dialect.

A crossbow cost about two hundred dollars, (around ten thousand rupees). In this game, the target is set on an earthen mound and then the archers try to aim at it from a distance of 12 feet. There is no specific condition for the participants, just about anybody, young or old, can take part in it. This game does not require any special ground or stadium even and can be organised in any open ground.

Ziauddin said to Malala: "If the government supports this game giving it official recognition, it could become all the more popular. It is played in five-six districts of Khyber Pakhtunkhwah, but this is not so popular because the government pays no attention to it. There is no specific ground for it, nor is there any financial aid."

"But, Father, this game should be brought up at the national level, shouldn't it?"

"Of course, Malala, but this game is organised between different districts of the area despite all these limitations, and hundreds of people gather to watch this game."

"It must be like a fair then, Father."

"Yes, why not..., and do you know that this programme is also includes with music for recreation."

"Father, will any such thing ever occur in our Mingora?" Ziauddin had no words to respond to her query; he was unsure when Swat would embrace the past glory, if ever it would.

Visit to Bunir was like a gust of pleasant and cool wind in the terror-filled life of Malala. On her return to the valley, she felt fresh and vigorous, like before. She told and retold her friends different stories of Bunir.

It was ninth of January. Yet another thing that occurred on this day was that the girls engaged themselves in a protracted debate over the information pertaining to the death of Maulana Shah Dauran, the Taliban spokesman on the FM channel. It was he who had announced the ban on girls' going to school.

Some girls claimed that he had died, while others did not agree with this. This suspense arose because he did not speak on the radio on the previous night, so his death became a rumour amongst people. One girl claimed that he had gone on a holiday. All this light talk made Malala feel as if their past days were there again.

The winter vacation was fast approaching, the school was about to be closed. This time, the school headmistress declared the vacation but did not specify the dates when the vacation would end. This had occurred for the first time. The girls thought that this had been done following the Taliban's edict to ban girls from going to school after the fifteenth of January.

Malala and her friends were not at all happy, as they used to be in the past. They thought that if the Taliban enforced its edict, maybe they would never be able to visit school ever again. Of course, some girls hoped that the school would resume in February again. Others said that their parents had preferred to change the place to continue their education.

This was the last day of the school, so Malala and her friends decided to play in the school playground until late. Malala hoped that the school would not be closed down, but when she set out back home, she looked back at the school building with curious and eager eyes as if it was for the last time she was looking at it.

On this day, Malala delivered a very sentimental speech to the girls. She made them vow that they would give their life but would not stop coming to school. Her father Ziauddin had been participating in social and community programmes for long; the open-minded teacher had been opposing the Taliban's *firmans* in the name of Sharia law. Malala had adopted her father's sentiments as well as his style too quickly.

All this while, the whole of Swat resonated with the military troops. The entire valley would tremble with the sound of gunfire and explosions. It was during this period that the local newspapers carried articles regarding Malala's diary. When people discussed with her father about those articles, he found it impossible to reveal to them that Gul Makai was none else but his own daughter.

During the military action, the government came to the forefront to ensure girls' security to school, but the guardians were still unsure. They were not ready to send their girls to school until the Taliban retracted its announcement on the FM channel. All of them said that their education had been interrupted only because of the military. Swat was under the influence of so much terror that even the boys' schools which fell in the route of the military convoys were closed down.

The schools gave a deserted look during the vacation; and then news came that five schools had been bombed; one of these was close to Malala's house. She wondered why the schools had been destroyed when they were already closed. Nobody had ever stepped into schools after the Taliban's deadline. Why did these people punish the school buildings? Her friends intimated her that possibly the schools had been burnt down in rage because Maulana Shah Dauran's uncle had been murdered a few days before.

Malala wondered how the Taliban could have destroyed their schools for something they had not done. And she wondered why the military was not able to protect them. Why? Why was it so?

Malala was unable to get answers to many of her queries, so she would turn to her diary to tell them what was happening around her. Now the schools were completely shut down. Many of her friends had gone out of Swat with their families. To her despair, the Mulla Radio issued another *firman* ordering girls not to go out of the house. He also announced that his fighters would destroy any school which was taken by the army as their post.

Malala was informed by her father that the army had garrisoned in the girls' and boys' high schools in Haji Baba. On the other hand, Maulana Shah Dauran said in his announcement on the radio that three thieves would be punished with lashes the following day, and anyone willing to see the act could reach the square. Malala and other people were stunned at this announcement. They wondered why people went to watch such acts when so much of oppression was being thrust upon them. From all the information that Malala had, she could infer that there would be Taliban where the army was, but there would not be any army where the Taliban was.

Education was adversely affected for girls like Malala, and the centres of higher education too were not untouched by this menace. A professor of the Swat Medical College at Mingora informed Ziauddin: "The Taliban have banned students from attending the practical classes being conducted in the gynaecology ward or delivery room."

"How do you give these students training in practical?" asked Ziauddin.

"The situation is really grave. We could not have done so even if we wished to because the Taliban has started to send its representatives to the medical college, so that they can ensure that their prohibition was being complied with," the professor informed sorrowfully.

"But you can't sit with fingers crossed at this situation, can you? You will have to find some way."

"Yes, we have found out a way," he murmured in a hushed voice. "We are conducting gynaecology classes in another district, and now there is a proposal to shift the college elsewhere."

"Oh! It would cause a great misery to the people of Mingora."

"Of course, it would, but we can't play with the students' future either." The professor was right.

Ziauddin could see that Malala laying/staying at home the whole day thinking of her past days at school, she actively thought if she would ever be able to appear in the examinations or not. It was the last week of January 2009, but they little knew if the school would reopen or not, or if the girls could resume their studies even if the school opened.

By the time army had reached, dozens of schools had been destroyed and hundreds of others shut down. Had they taken action at the adequate time, the situation would not have gone out of control. She had a bad thought. She was afraid that the schools under the army protection would be attacked by the Taliban fighters; it would make the children even more wary of the army's presence in the school.

One day, the helicopters dropped candies and toffees to children below in order to enhance cooperation between the local population and the army, and this continued over many days. It made Malala, her brother and other children of the locality to come out in the open whenever they heard helicopter flying about and wait for the candies. But gradually, this ceased. The situation in Swat was growing unstable, but Ziauddin did not want to shift from Mingora. However, keeping the circumstances in view, he decided to leave for Islamabad. It made his three children very happy. Malala was going to Islamabad for the first time, she was very curious about it. Meanwhile, her diary was being continuously broadcast on the BBC.

Malala was aware that the Taliban terrorists searched passengers on the way, so she was very scared but was happy that no such thing happened with her. Rather the army searched them. When Swat was left behind, they all felt relieved, their terror evaporated into thin air. They all stayed with a friend of Ziauddin.

Swat is replete with natural beauty, but she found artificial beauty of Islamabad equally good.

Now, she was growing, so Toorpekai started to mould her as per the customs and traditions prevalent in Swat. She impressed upon her to wear yashmak, which Malala called 'shuttle cock', she never liked to wear it. Ziauddin too stood in her favour and said: "Veil or shame lies in the eyes, and in the soul, what use is the external veil?"

Whenever they were out of the house, her mother would ask her to cover her face as some man was gazing at her.

At this, Malala would laugh, "Let him, Mother, after all, I am seeing him too."

Staying in Islamabad Malala remembered the paternal village of Barkana. Normally, they got an opportunity to visit the village on Eid. This was very exciting time for her, she scarcely slept at night waiting to go there. It took them four to five hours to arrive in the village. They took a bus from Mingora early in the morning. They also carried with them all that they could not get in the village. Malala loved to watch natural scenery, spread all around, so she liked to sit on the window without worrying for the dust storm that the bus raised moving on the dusty narrow roads along the rice fields on the hills and reached Shangla. In this region of the valley are located three villages: Barkana (paternal village), Karsat (maternal village) and there is Shahpur. When they reached here, Ziauddin and her brothers would stay at Barkana, while Malala and Toorpekai would stay at Karsat. Malala stayed there because she loved the company of her nieces Anisa and Sambul. Moreover the house was made from brick and mortar, together with bath facility. The prayer times in the villages are normally decided as per the position of the sun. This village fell in the category of poor villages, but whenever she visited, a fine feast was served to them. Food was cooked by women. There were plenty of rice, chicken and milk. No child had any toys or books, the boys would play cricket with a plastic ball. Malala was born in an urban area, so she was not fully acquainted with the life in village. The village women would often ask Malala, "Will you cook chicken for us?"

Malala would say in response: "Hens are very innocent, I cannot murder them."

Village women keep their faces covered with the yashmak and are forbidden to talk to a stranger. Therefore, when a relative saw Malala wearing fashionable clothes and uncovered face, he enquired of her father why she did not veil her face.

Ziauddin said: "She is my daughter, I know what is good or bad for her; you should better not interfere in such things."

Listening to such contention, the rustic people took them for modern people, and some families started criticizing them too that they were no more any Pashtuns.

However, it was during her sojourn at Islamabad when she came to know how backward they were considered by the city people.

The struggle in Swat benefited Malala and her brothers only this much that they could jump over the boundaries of Mingora to visit different places. They went to Peshawar from Islamabad. There, they had tea with a relative; after this they intended to go to Banu.

Atal, Malala's younger brother, was five years old then. He was playing in the courtyard of the house, when Ziauddin asked him: "What are you doing, child?"

He said: "I am making graves for the Taliban terrorists."

Everybody broke out in a loud laughter, but Ziauddin grew serious. He was restless to know the negative impact terrorism had on the innocent child.

Not long after, they all left for Banu by wagon; it was old and its driver often honked it. Once the wagon got trapped in a pit on the road and the driver happened to press horn this time too. At this, Kushhal suddenly woke up frightenedly from sleep and asked, "Has explosion occured". He was looking around in astonishment.

The children's minds were haunted by bombs, explosions, corpses and army; they were being chased by bad dreams day and night.

By the nightfall, they arrived at Banu, where Ziauddin's friends awaited them. They too were Pashtuns, but their dialect was Binusi, which children could not follow. Banu was more peaceful than Swat, though the Taliban had its presence there too. The condition had not deteriorated so much here. The Taliban had threatened to close down girls' schools, but it had no impact here.

Malala and her family were out of Swat for the last four days. Now, Ziauddin thought of returning home, so he headed for Peshawar. While on the way, Malala got a telephone call from a friend in Swat, who was extremely terrified. She said that the situation was very grave and advised her not to return to Swat. She informed that the military operation was intensive, and thirty-seven people had died of mortar shells.

This information made them anxious. When they reached Peshawar in the evening, they switched on the television to know the current situation despite their fatigue. They were stunned at what they saw. The news pertained to Swat, where people could be seen fleeing from Swat. People walked on windy dusty roads empty-handed.

Malala was filled with remorse. She thought that there was a time when many people from other cities and countries visited Swat for entertainment, but now the people of Swat were forced to flee from there.

In anxiety, Malala switched to another channel, on which a woman was saying: "We will take revenge for every drop of blood that the martyr Benazir Bhutto shed."

At this, Malala asked her father sitting nearby: "Abbu, tell me one thing. Who will revenge for the blood of hundreds of people of Swat?"

Ziauddin had no answer to this question. He could guess that Malala was eager about her school and education, and her fear came true. In the next few days, she came to know that it was proclaimed to keep even boys' schools closed up to 8 February.

Ziauddin came to know that this notice had been put up on private boys' schools which meant that they would reopen on the ninth, but no such notice had been put up on the girls' schools, which meant that Malala's and her friends' school would not open any more. There was a time when girls were hopeful that the school will reopen after the winter break. Now that happiness was lost and they were afraid that their school might be closed forever at the Taliban's injunction.

Ziauddin postponed his return to Swat. Then they decided to send Toorpekai and Kushhal to Swat first; and twenty days later, Malala, Atal and Ziauddin too travelled to Mingora.

Homecoming is an hour of pleasure, but this was conjoined with a sense of fear too. When they entered Mingora and passed through Kambar area, they found the area strangely desolated and deserted. They could find no people other than a few men with long beards and hair. From their appearance, they looked like the Talibanis. Malala could see some houses riddled with bullets.

At Mingora, they did not find this place as pleasant as it used to be. Before making to their home, they went to the Shah Super Market, which used to be open late in the night, but now it was all closed. The three did not tell about their return to Mingora because they wanted to surprise Toorpekai and Kaushhal and they of course succeeded in this. Toorpekai was pleasantly surprised to have them there.

But more than Toorpekai, they themselves were surprised, not pleasantly of course because they could not see many of their valuable articles in the house. During this vacation, a theft had deprived them of all those things. Earlier, such thefts never occurred in the area but such incidents often took place after the situation deteriorated.

Toorpekai thanked God and said: "Thank Heavens that we had neither cash nor gold at house."

"But Ammi," said Malala looking for her bracelets and anklets, "I can't find them here."

"Maybe the thieves have taken them for gold," said her mother. Malala was not happy at this. Later she found articles elsewhere in the house. Maybe the thieves took them but soon could make out that they were not made of gold, so they threw them.

Malala wanted to go to school, but she was forbidden. Boys' schools had opened. She would often open her cupboard and curse her fate on seeing her uniform, schoolbag and geometry box. She murmured when all boys' sections were open in private schools, what the problem was with girls' education. Why? What is our crime? Is there no one to give us justice on this land? Whose evil glance has befallen this land of Swat? People are completely terrorized, where is their smile, their laughter? What can I do that I may restore their smile? She asked herself.

Thinking this, she picked up and opened her geometry box. She found two hundred rupees in it. This money was the fine that she had collected from girls in the school for their absence or late-coming. Her teacher had assigned her the responsibility of collecting such fines. These notes seemed to make faces at her: "Take money from everybody for absence...you too are absent from school now!"

She also noticed her blackboard marker in the cupboard...she recalled many things about her school, the most she thought about were the quarrels with her classmates.

Kushhal's school was about to open the next day but he had not done his homework even a bit, so he was unnerved and did not want to go to school. Just then, news came that curfew could be imposed from the following day, this made him burst into a gay dance. Seeing him dancing, Malala felt even more sorrowful, she wanted to burst out crying: "Send me to school! I want to go to school!" But who could she tell this? Everybody knew how restless and desperate she was.

Malala listened to the sounds the school-going children made outside; they were not many, still those were heading to school who could go. Boys' schools had been opened, and girls too started to go to school after the Taliban lifted their ban on primary classes. There were both boys and girls in Kushhal's school up to the fifth grade.

Kushhal returned from school to inform that only six children, including only one girl were present in the class out of a total of forty-nine. There were only about seventy children in the assembly out of a total of seven hundred.

When Malala was away to Islamabad, the theft in her house also caused them the loss of television. She had nothing to do at home now. She sometimes tuned to the Mulla Radio, which kept parroting the edicts of Maulana Fazlullah. This kept terrorizing the people more and more. One night, she heard on the FM channel Maulana saying in these terms: "The suicide attack on the police station in Mingora should be understood only a pressure cooker explosion; this will be followed by a cauldron explosion, and in the end, there will be a tanker explosion."

At night, Ziauddin narrated Malala all that was happening in Swat. She noticed that everybody talked more frequently of troops, Taliban, rocket, arson, firing, shelling, Maulana Fazlullah, Muslim Khan, police, helicopter, died, wounded and so on. Once there was a time when people recreated themselves with light programmes on the television but now the Taliban had prohibited the cable television so she could not watch her favourite programme on the Star Plus: *Raja ki Ayegi Baraat*. Malala loved comedy, like any other child. She also loved to watch a comic programme on the Pakistani channel Zio: *Ham Sab Ummid Se Hain*. But now, all this had ceased beyond redemption; there was silence, stillness, quietness everywhere around.

The same day, Malala heard the elders talking that most attacks occurred on Fridays, only because the suicide bombers thought that it was a sacred day in Islam, and it would beget him more blessings if he attacked on this day. This was shocking for her, because it was Friday. She could not sleep at night, her mind was filled to the brim with scare, fright, terror; she was restless, uneasy, desperate. She picked up her pen and started jotting down her terror in the diary as Gul Makai. This told the world how people of Swat lived under the dark shadow of terror. It was a Friday in the mid-February. When she left the bed in the morning, her mother informed that somebody had murdered a rickshaw-puller and an old watchman. These people could not have done anything bad to anyone. Why were they murdered? Malala asked herself, but was devoid of any answer.

Life in Swat was turning from bad to worse. Hundreds of people from the surrounding areas arrived in Mingora, while the people of Mingora were fleeing to other towns. The prosperous went out of Swat, and the poor had nowhere to go but to suffer the fate there itself.

In such a scaring atmosphere, Malala telephoned Tayazad, a cousin and asked him to come with the vehicle as she wanted to go round Mingora. When they went out, she found that all markets were closed and roads deserted.

The army had seized Swat completely and they were trapping the Taliban terrorists gradually which resulted into clashes on daily basis. Towards the close of February, Malala's family had relatives from Peshawar and other villages nearby. When they were having lunch, it started firing outside. Malala had never experienced such heavy shelling before. All of them were completely frightened thinking that the Taliban had surrounded them. Malala scurried to her father to seek protection, who soothed her saying: "Don't be afraid, this is firing is for peace."

He further informed her: "The morning newspaper said that dialogue between the government and the Taliban is underway for restoring peace, and this has made people jubilant, so they are firing."

The news filtered in that Amir Hussain Hoti, the province's chief minister had said that the government had done everything that it could do and it had appealed to the Taliban to lay down arms.

It was in this connection that the Loya Zirga was being held in Swat under the leadership of Sufi Mohammad. On the other hand, the Taliban asserted that they would consider ceasing their action permanently only after they had considered the document.

Sufi Mohammad said: "We are talking with the government on a 22-point demand charter. There was disagreement on five points, which have been removed from the forthcoming meeting."

And the same evening, the FM radio announced ceasefire. It led to even more intensive firing, as people believed the Taliban more than the government. When this news reached Malala's house, her mother started crying, so did Ziauddin and her two younger brothers.

It was 15th February 2009, when the Taliban announced a ten-day ceasefire in the Swat valley. A Taliban spokesman said that this step had been initiated in good faith due to the ongoing peace process between the government and their organisation. Under this good faith, they also released a Chinese Engineer who had been kidnapped earlier.

Muslim Khan, spokesman for the Taliban, spoke to the media thus: "We are announcing a unilateral ceasefire for ten days owing to the recent developments, but we can violate the ceasefire if we are attacked."

Those days, foreigners were being attacked in the Swat valley. Just about those days, a Polish geologist had been murdered. Jon Soleski, an American and UN officer, had been kidnapped from this area. The kidnappers issued a video in which they threatened to hack him to death within seventy-two hours.

When Malala got up the following morning, she was happy in view of restoration of peace. She noticed that the helicopter was flying at a low altitude. A cousin of hers commented that with the onset of peace, the helicopters had started to fly low. By afternoon, the entire Swat resonated with the news of restoration of peace; people were happy, sweets were distributed. A friend rang up Malala to congratulate her saying that she would get an opportunity to set foot outside the four walls of the house, as she had been closed within a room for the past few months. They were happy that the girls' schools could reopen.

By mid-February, the town regained its luster and crowdedness. Malala and her friends were extremely happy, they once again started to prepare for their examinations;

they now hoped that the schools would be reopened after the restoration of peace.

The children had already been affected by the terror that prevailed in Swat. Malala could feel this fact. The favourite game for her younger brothers was the fight between the army and the Taliban. One would act as if dropping bombs from helicopter while the other would fire at the helicopter with a paper gun. She heard her brother say that he would like to make an atom bomb. She did not know whether to laugh or scream at her brother.

That day, Maulana Sufi Mohammad, chief of Taliban, arrived in Swat. It appeared as if the entire media thronged Swat. When asked about it, Ziauddin told Malala that he had come there to establish peace. His arrival made the town more crowded, the market was alive with activity. Malala raised her hands to pray for the success of peace talks, for she hoped that it would at least lead to opening of girls' schools.

However, nothing of the sort happened. The next day in the evening, Malala's father informed her that Musa Khan, a journalist from Swat, had been murdered by some anonymous man. Listening to this, her mother felt unwell. Their hopes for restoration of peace had been belied. The house was swept in a wave of despair.

The 28-year-old Musa Khan was a sports journalist, but was here to report about the entourage of Sufi Mohammad. He was working for the Zio television channel. He was killed in Matta area of Swat, which was immensely influenced by the Taliban. He had gone to Matta for reporting. People had seen him there too. However, while on his way back, some unknown people kidnapped him and first riddled his body with thirty-two bullets, and when they were not satisfied with this, they hacked down his head. Musa Khan was assigned the responsibility of reporting about the Taliban, ISI and Pakistani Swat. In his last message, he communicated that he had come to possess some very vital information, which he was going to place before the world in the evening. This message is clear enough to tell that he had some shocking news, a piece of breaking news, but he had been done away with before he could do it.

The local journalists sat in protest at the square with his dead body. In the past three years, three journalists had been killed in the area.

Toorpekai did not want to tell any news in the house which could wrap it in the clouds of graver terror. Listening to this, Malala said to her brothers that from then on, they would rather play a peace game in place of the war game. Despite the poor condition, the schools endeavoured to ensure that the girls did not lose their year, so they announced to hold examinations of the girls' sections from the first week of March.

Two days later, Ziauddin brought happy news, he said that the Taliban had lifted the ban on girls' schools. This occurred on 21 February 2009. Swat was regaining its composure gradually. The use of firing and bomb explosions diminished in scale. However, the people were still terrorized, lest the peace talks. There were rumours that some Taliban commanders were not ready to accept this, they claimed to fight until the last.

Such rumours shook everybody. Malala asked herself why they were bent upon doing so. The Taliban commanders said that they wanted to wreak vengeance for the Jamia Hafsa and Lal Masjid. What were the common people to blame for all this?

"Abbu, what is the matter of Jamia Hafsa and Lal Masjid?" one day Malala asked her father.

He told her that the Lal Masjid (Red Mosque) or Jama Masjid was a mosque in Ghaziabad Lakaro in Islamabad, Pakistan's capital. It is one of the oldest mosques in the country. A religious madrasa for women and a Jamia Faridia Madrasa for boys are affiliated to this mosque.

The Lal Masjid was built in 1965, and it was so named after its red walls and interiors. Maulana Abdullah was appointed its first Imam. In 1998, Maulana Mohammad Abdullah was murdered, and he was succeeded by Abdul Aziz Ghazi and Abdul Rashid Ghazi; and this led to making it a centre of fundamentalist teaching and open opposition to the government.

In 2007, the Taliban supporter of the Mohammad tribal area took over the control of the Jama Masjid at Ghaziabad Lakaro.

About 150 masked men were deployed on the outer side of the mosque, and renamed the mosque as Lal Masjid. It was also reported that an adjacent girls' madrasa too was taken under control, and its name was changed to Jamia Hafsa.

Malala heard all this in disbelief. She asked, "Then?"

Her father continued to narrate: "And then, the military operation had to be carried out for a week. The Pakistani army started its action after seizing the mosque one morning, and this conflict continued for thirty-six hours. After this terrible fighting, they recovered 73 dead bodies from the premises of the mosque, including that of Abdul Rashid Ghazi, the fundamentalist leader."

"Oh, I see!"

Ziauddin took a long breath and then said: "You might know that the Lal Masjid has been in headlines for one or the other negative cause. For the past several months, the Pakistan Government is in conflict with the Lal Masjid and students of the two madrasas affiliated to it on several issues. The religious leaders of the mosque demand that the Islamic Sharia law should be imposed in the capital of Pakistan."

"What has the Lal Masjid to do in this controversy, Abbu?"

"It is so connected because the *Talib* or scholars are connected with it. This mosque came into headlines for the first time when the students of the madrasas raided a

Chinese beauty parlour and kidnapped nine people from there, including six Chinese girls. The present impasse started from third of July when the students of the mosque took to roads, and the security forces had to use teargas shells to disperse them. After this, some students went on to fire some rounds from the inside, which killed a troop. After this, it was surrounded from all sides, and in the ensuing firing, ten people were killed. The government asked the students to lay down their arms, the mosque was seized and electricity supply was snapped."

"How many people were there?"

"According to administration's estimate, there were somewhere between two to five thousand people in the mosque at this time. That day, more than 700 students surrendered themselves. The rapidly changing scenario led to the arrest of Maulana Abdul Aziz, who was trying to flee in the garb of a yashmak."

"Then?" Malala grew curious.

"From the third morning after the deadlock, the Pakistani army started its operation. By the 3rd day, about sixteen people had died and about 1200 people had surrendered. It was still feared that there were a large number of people still inside. Abdul Rashid Ghazi said that he was ready for surrender with the condition that no action would be taken inside the mosque. However, the government declined to accept this demand."

"It was done right, it should have been so," Malala gave her frank opinion.

"And then on the next day, that is, on 6 July, the army operation continued, some relaxation was given to allow the women to come out. No direct attack was launched on the people inside the mosque. It was aimed to make the fundamentalists surrender. The number of the dead rose to 21 in four days."

"Wasn't our government doing anything?"

"It was doing everything but the deadlock continued on the 5th day too that was 7th of July. President Parvez Musharraf warned the students inside the mosque to surrender else they would be killed in the ongoing operations. At this time, the army tanks were deployed outside the mosque but the *Tajib* were in no mood to relent, so conflict took place on the 8th day once again. The army exploded the walls of the mosque to allow the women out and terrible fighting broke out between troops and students. A colonel died in this firing."

"It was a bad thing to happen."

"Of course, it was and so on the next day, 9th of July, Parvez Musharraf constituted a special team, comprising the former Prime Minister Shujat Hussain to end the impasse. This team talked to those inside through loudspeaker, but of no avail. On the other hand, the Supreme Court of Pakistan ordered not to stop the military operation.

"The talks led to no result and the Pakistani army, when on the 8th day the talks failed, started its action from the morning hours. This action claimed the lives of about 50 Taliban terrorists and eight troops; however, the greatest success for the army was the shooting down of Abdul Rashid Ghazi, the chief manager of the Lal Masjid."

"I can understand that the *Talibs* want to take revenge for that now."

"No doubt, this was the reason that the *Talibs* announced from the mosque loudspeaker that they would keep fighting against America and its allied countries. A *talib* named Khalid said in his interaction with the media that they would continue with the mission of the deceased Maulana Abdul Rashid Ghazi and his martyrdom would not go futile."

"Abbu, I ask a simple question. Why don't they take revenge from the people who undertook this operation? Why have we to suffer for this?" Ziauddin had no word to say in response to these questions. He himself thought about this question several times but had no answer.

All people heaved a sigh of relief when Maulana Fazlullah announced on the FM radio: "We take back our decision so far as it pertains to the ban on girls' schools. Girls can go to school until examinations which are beginning from seventeen March, but they will have to use the veil."

Malala jumped in joy to listen to this; she never believed if this could happen ever again. However, she and her theology teacher were not happy with wearing the yashmak. The teacher had to wear it out of fear of the Taliban, and she explained this thing to Malala too, who was too stubborn to follow this edict. She said that the Taliban wished to hide their identity by concealing women behind veils, but she would rise to protest against it.

Malala was extremely happy on 23 February when she set out for school. Only a few girls were in school uniform, the others were in civil clothes scared of any untoward incident. They were afraid that the Taliban terrorists could kidnap them or throw acid on their faces. Such things were quite common for them to do. Most girls hugged one another in the assembly, and they were all very happy.

At the end of the assembly, the headmistress said: "You should be particular about covering your faces, and you must wear yashmaks, because the Taliban has attached this condition as necessary for girls to go to school."

That day, only twelve girls of her class attended school as some had already left Swat, while there were others who were not allowed by their parents to attend school. Four of Malala's friends had already left Swat and one was about to go to Rawalpindi. Malala advised this friend to stay back as peace had been restored and the condition was returning to normalcy gradually however, her friend said that she hardly trusted all that.

Four of her friends had already left, and she was left with only one, who too was going away soon.

When Malala saw that her friends were not attending the school, she motivated other students of the school not to stop attending school, and stand against the terrorists bravely, but she did not succeed in her mission. She often visited their houses for this purpose.

The examinations started from 9 March, so she was busy in her studies for most of the time. Asif Ali Zardari, the then President, signed a controversial ordinance which provided for a complicated system of Shariat law in the Swat region. This ordinance was supported by Sufi Mohammad, the founder of Tehrik-e-Shariat-e-Mohammadi. This Talibani group had been active for a long time now. He issued a *firman*: "From now on, women will neither go to the market nor jobs."

It was after this that the government and the Taliban came face to face again. Mingora was being evacuated, and with this the Yousafzai family had to migrate from there. Ziauddin went to Peshawar to protest against this, while Malala with her mother and brothers went to Shangla to stay with relatives. Shangla is a rural area where no degree college exists even today. Malala did not like the area as there she had no books to read.

The Swat valley witnessed armed struggle between the army and Taliban fighters continuously for three months. The number of flags seen in the valley far exceeded even those that were hoisted in Karachi on the national Independence day. At this time, the army vehicles used to go round the streets playing the Pakistani anthem loudly.

The local people opposed the presence of army in such a large number. They opined that the situation would continue to be uncertain until the army was present there. The situation could improve if all the powers were handed over to the local administration; however, the danger would have still persisted. People were afraid of the army, and the local people fled whenever they saw an army vehicle approaching.

Every person of the town had been a victim of the army's violence in one or the other way. The army had arrested and shot dead a number of people. They were so frightened of the army that they did not raise their voices even when the commodities in the market were being sold at very inflated prices.

Common people wont to speak about neither Taliban terrorists, nor army. Both of them had unleashed terror in order to maintain their supremacy; and such a situation could not be found anywhere else in Pakistan than in Swat.

The schools started again, it was the matter that the Taliban was staunchly against. In 2009, the Pakistani army gained its control over Swat, and then the Prime Minister announced that people could now return to Swat. After this, on 24 July 2009, Malala returned to Mingora.

□

5
Open Opposition to Taliban

Malala had been very clear about her goal right since the beginning. She was a clear-headed girl, she knew what she ought to do under a particular situation. Therefore, she had already made up her mind during this free time what she would have to do to fight against the atrocities being let loose by the *Talibs*. She did not sit idly after her return. She participated in one or the other activity until the last. In 2009, children from different schools were participating in the District Child Assembly, founded by the Khapal Kor Foundation and run by the funds released by the UNICEF. Malala was invited to attend this as the chairperson. Malala

addressed the assembly, which had primarily been founded to raise voice in connection with children's rights. She said: "We will have to reconstruct our those schools which the Taliban has destroyed. There are thousands of children who don't go to school, but the government has failed to pay attention to this aspect. Though the situation in the Swat valley is changing after the military action. New schools are being constructed, yet I think that all this should materialize as soon as possible, as it would be quite difficult to study in tents both in summer and winter."

Malala was extremely determined. She had attraction and depth in her voice, and blended with clear thinking made her a favourite with all people.

When Adam B. Ellick, a video journalist, heard Malala speaking before hundreds of children, he decided to make a documentary on her. He stayed with her and her family for six months in order to see the effect of the Taliban on daily life in the Swat valley. The documentary was in two parts. The first part was based on how her father was forced to shut down his private school, and how Malala's education was disrupted. This part, titled *Class Dismissed,* depicted the misery inflicted on the schools by the Taliban in a very heartrending manner. In the second part was depicted how Malala's family had to migrate after the military action.

This documentary brought Malala's recognition to become an international voice for women's education. At the end of the film, Adam showed how Malala was seeking help from the representatives of Pakistani, Afghan and American presidents. The rise of a little girl before the fearsome Taliban that had crushed education in the valley, clearly showed that she could not be pressurized by anything. This documentary made Malala popular outside Pakistan too. The international community now paid attention to her; it brought to light the frightening situation that Malala and other young girls had to face in Pakistan.

Meanwhile, Malala started to take part in the *Open Minds Project* held by the Institute for War and Peace Reporting. The goal of this project was to start journalism training in Pakistan's 42 schools and to arrive at some decision after discussion on the current affairs. Malala had created a niche for herself owing to her clear thinking, and many people had been attached to the project after her encouragement. Her popularity led to inviting her on television shows. While speaking to Hami Mir, the star anchor of Zio television, Malala said: "I want to study the law and enter politics. I have dreamt of a country where education is the predominant factor." She was feeling relieved after the small bans by the Taliban had been lifted away.

Malala spoke in favour of open views in all her interviews. The media gave her so much of importance that she seemed to have become a symbol of open thinking in Pakistan. Her relatives opined that she was still too young to understand the importance of leftist or rightist politics, it was her father who had shaped her views. Ziauddin wished that her daughter should come to the fore in the Swat valley as a girl possessing open views. He himself was considered a social worker having open views, and he was the chairman of an organisation called Global Peace and spokesperson of the Swat Aman Zirge (Swat Peace Assembly). Both these organisations contributed significantly in efforts of maintaining peace in Swat.

In October 2011, Desmond Tutu nominated Malala for the International Children Peace Prize, which made her a popular face not only in the country but abroad also. The Nobel Award winner Michaela of South Africa, in Amsterdam, Holland, nominated Malala with 90 other participants. He said in this function: "Malala has displayed courage to stand for herself and other girls, and she has used the national and international media in order to tell to the world that girls too have the right to go to school."

This award was not given to Malala this time, but the nomination for it brought her name and fame. At that time, the 13-year-old Malala got the status of a celebrity. Malala felt no disappointment when she was not chosen for this award. Rather, she said that Mackala, a special child, was fully eligible to be the winner of the award and encouraged her. As her identity was revealed internationally, she became the brave Malala, but she was now like a thorn in the eyes of the Taliban. Her father was one of those who were making effort to protect Swat from the Taliban, so the entire family became a target of the Taliban. All this while, Malala was, on 19 December 2011, given the National Peace Award, instituted for the first time for the Pakistani youths by the government.

Later speaking to the media, Malala expressed her intention to form a political party aimed at education. She expressed anguish at her pen and books being snatched away from her, and said that the daughters of Swat were scared of no one even after the Taliban's *firmans*. This was clear enough from the fact that the girls in Swat continued with their education despite all the bans. Honouring her courage, the government girls' secondary school at Mission Road was renamed Malala Yousafzai Government Girls' Secondary School. On her request, Prime Minister Gilani ordered to create an IT camp in the Swat Degree College for Women.

Now, the real identity of Gul Makai was brought to the open who was behind the Urdu blog of the BBC; the Pakistani television news channels showed that she was none else but Malala who has been honoured with the National Peace Prize by the government, nominated for an international award and given prominence at public places as a spokesperson of girls' right to education.

All this enraged the Taliban still further. The Taliban was worried that Malala was having a positive impact on

other girls too. They were worried that this impact influenced not only the girls but also the men in their families. The Taliban mentioned such a conduct on the part of Malala as shamelessness and a symbol of Western civilisation. Several orthodox Muslims were scared of her popularity, fame and power, while Islam says that everybody should be given education as per his or her wish. In such a situation, Malala proved to be a role model for other girls too. The Taliban thought that she was an American agent and termed her a rebel who had challenged the Pashto tradition; who had violated the Shariat law, and who used to provide the BBC with information pertaining to the Mujahiddin and Taliban. It claimed that she used cosmetics while going for interviews, her insane father had made her insane too, and so it said that they would first kill Malala and then her father.

Malala and her father started receiving threats; stones were hurled at her house and school, but Malala was not ready to give up. In addition to writing diary, she also started her campaign for girls' education in the valley. Wherever she went, she said that death was certain, it must come one day, but what was the logic behind dying a cowardly death? The speeches by this little girl started to reach out to the world, as Gul Makai, through the BBC, had become a synonym for revolution against the Taliban. As this brave girl became a talking point, the Taliban was cautioned, it threatened the school Principal, but Malala was not ready to retract from her stand and activities.

The relatives and other acquaintances tried to explain that it was in her own interest to remain in veil and stop from speaking publicly, but she opposed this advice saying: "The burqa is not my identity, my face is my identity, and I will not hide this behind a yashmak." Looking at her determination, the government offered her security, but Ziauddin rejected this offer. He said that the school environment could not remain normal under the shadow of guns. Despite all this, Malala was not scared, she continued to hold her post. She stuck to her mission with all enthusiasm.

School vacation was round the corner. Like always, Ziauddin had planned to take students for an excursion to the waterfall at Margajar. This plan delighted the girls as they remembered greenery spread in the valley with streams of cool water and fragrance of flowers. Malala and her friends were extremely happy at this plan. Just about this time, a pamphlet was thrown in the school, it said: "You people are degrading the character of our girls, and are taking them out on a picnic. It amounts to vulgarity as they would wander there without a veil."

Ziauddin, nevertheless, was not scared. He took all girls to Margajar, where they were very happy breathing in the free air.

One day in wee hours, somebody knocked at Malala's house. Ziauddin was disturbed from sleep. He felt as if some Taliban terrorists had attacked his place. However, he felt easy after he found his brother Akeel instead. But his brother was worried. He glanced outside anxiously to ensure that no one was chasing him. At such a situation, Ziauddin asked him: "What's the matter with you? Is everything well at home?"

"We're all right, brother, but it's Malala's life that you should worry about," said Akeel. "I entreat you to check her from speaking publicly. If you can't do this, or if she doesn't agree to do this, just leave the place with her. Her life is in danger. Her talks are inciting people, and all this has made to the Taliban, and they could attack anytime to get rid of this innocent girl."

Akeel stammered saying all this. He was not within himself when he uttered these words. Listening to the sounds, Malala too woke up. She was happy to find her uncle there, but then her father said: "Malala, your uncle advises that we must leave this place."

Malala was not moved at this, rather she said: "Abbu, my uncle is a nice man, but his advice doesn't go well with bravery."

Malala was a well-known name all around. As the time ticked by, history found itself manifest in 2012 when the Talibani sharpshooters kept an eye over her daily routine; they noted whom all she met, when she left for school, when she came back, what all she did after school and all.

□

6

Dreaded Day of 9 October

Even the throne finds itself in a far secondary role when confronted with the pen. When the pen inspires a revolution, even the strongest rulers taste dust overnight, and this brings into existence a golden history. When the dictatorship of Taliban terrorists had put off all lamps of hopes in the Swat valley of Pakistan, there was still a twinkling lamp of promise trying to spread its light among the sounds of gunfire. This little lamp, called Malala had lighted thousands of lamps in the valley strengthening hopes of freedom. Holding the flame of women's rights aloft, she awakened the world towards girls' education, and proved that she alone was more than enough to devastate the very base of the fundamentalist Taliban.

Malala was that firefly that lighted the entire valley suffering from the orthodox tribal customs and caste dogmas with hopes of some resurrection. The schools in Swat used to open when the Taliban wished them to, and were closed down at their command. It was the order of the day to bomb and shoot at schools. This was the reason that all dreams of girls for education, prospects and lives had all been crushed within a very narrow zone. Nobody had any anticipation what was coming three months after her fifteenth birthday. Her school was not very far from home, but the rapidly changing scenario compelled the worried Toorpekai to ask her to take a rickshaw in the morning and school bus in the afternoon. She concealed her real intentions and said: "Malala, you are grown up now, and it is advisable for you to take rickshaw from home and bus from school, it would ensure your safety."

It was the day of 9 October, it looked like any other day. Malala was heading home in the school van with her schoolmates. Like other days, the three-seated white Toyota van ran on the roads in the valley carrying twenty girls and three teachers. The road was desolate like it had become the norm there, only some people could be seen far and between. Malala sat with her best friends Moniba and Shazia Ramzan, and asked them: "There is no crowd on roads, is there? It looks so deserted."

She never knew what was going to occur the next moment. Once she had written somewhere: "I feel like throwing a shoe if I come across a Taliban terrorist, but I will not do so, else what will be the difference between him and me. I will rather request him to shoot me down, but not before listening to me. I must tell him that we have no personal enmity, I am raising my voice for the right of education that every school-going girl must get."

But nothing of the sort happened. When she was confronted with a Taliban terrorist, she did not find any time to express her views.

The van had scarcely moved about 100 yards when the girls watched from inside that Usman, the bus driver, braked. There were two youths standing in the middle of the road, they had their faces covered with handkerchiefs. A youth approached the bus driver and asked, "Does this bus belong to the Kushhal Public School?"

Usman thought what duffer he was, as the van bore the name of the school in big bold letters on the side. Still, he said, "Yes, it is."

"We want to know something about children," said the youth.

"You should better visit the school," said Usman.

While this youth was talking to the driver, the other one walked round. The girls could see the pistol peeping out from his belt. He climbed up, glanced at the girls and asked, "Who of you is Malala?"

All girls were out of their wits listening to the name of Malala who was sitting among them without a scarf. They thought for a while that he could be a journalist; and with this, all eyes turned to Malala, without a word. At this, Malala said, "It's I, Malala."

Listening to this, the masked man drew his black pistol and drew it at Malala. The girls screamed in horror. Malala held Moniba's hand, her grip tightened for a while, but then it loosened; for the youth had shot her thrice. One bullet pierced her left eye traversing through the skull to the shoulder. The second bullet hit Shazia at the left arm, while the third one touched past Shazia's left shoulder and set in at the top of right shoulder of Kaynat Rizvi who was sitting near her. Malala fell down unconscious in Moniba's lap. Blood oozed out from her temple and wetted Moniba's lap. Looking at blood, Kaynat too lost her sense.

The shooter was 23-year-old terrorist called Ataullah Khan, who fled from the scene after the shootout.

By the time people came to rescue, it was already ten minutes. The girls were crying in dread, while the driver drove to the Swat Central Hospital. The van was interrupted by a policeman, at this, a girl shouted: "O policeman, why should you waste our time? Malala is alive still. Let us go to hospital and run to catch that culprit who has done this evil act." Somehow, the policeman jumped aside while the van entered the hospital premises.

When they reached the hospital, Moniba was thought to be wounded owing to her blood-wetted clothes.

This incident spread in Mingora like a wildfire. When Ziauddin came to know of this, he was in the Press Club attending a meeting of the union of private schools in the Swat region. He was climbing up the stairs of the stage when

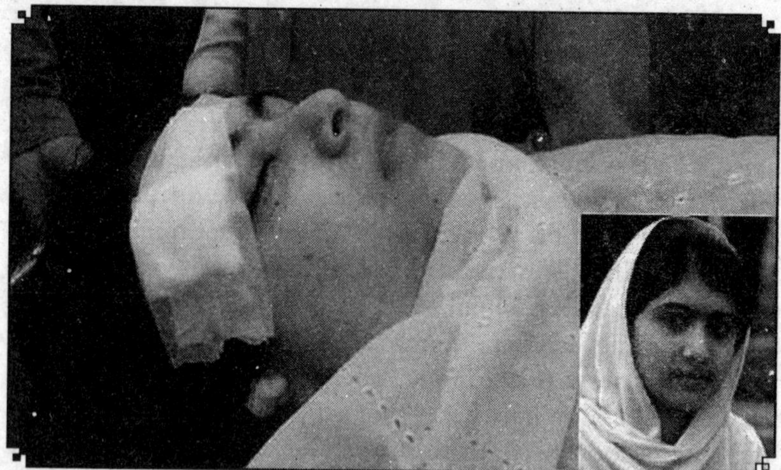

his mobile phone rang up. He saw that the call was from the Kushhal Public School, so he asked his friend Ahmad Shah to attend it, while he himself reached the mike to deliver the lecture. He had hardly held the mike when Ahmad Shah intimated him that the school van had been attacked by terrorists. Ziauddin's face lost its lustre in no time.

On this occasion, principals of about 400 private schools in the Swat valley had gathered to oppose imposition of the central regulatory authority on the private schools. Ziauddin was the president of the union, so he could not leave the meeting all of a sudden, else it could lead to disorder, so he continued with his speech. As no other man knew about the occurrence, he was not asked by anybody to leave.

He finished the speech somehow and, with the chairman's permission, hurried towards the hospital with his friend, Riyaz. It was just a five-minute drive from there. As he found the gathering cameramen and media persons thronging there, he was afraid if this attack was on no one else but Malala. He pierced through the crowd to enter the hospital only to find his darling Malala on the stretcher. He could not stop himself at her pitiable condition, he kissed her nose and cheek and said: "You are my brave daughter, I am proud of you, I take pride in you."

Malala's face showed a little sign of glow, which assured him that Malala was still alive.

Ziauddin was aware that any mishappening to Malala could mean like hitting two birds with one stone for the Taliban. He could have died grieving in case of her death. He was very scared, but he did not scream or cry. Whoever heard of the sorrowful news, he came running to the hospital. People raised their hands in prayers. Just about this time, Ziauddin received a call from the chief minister, who assured him and advised him to take Malala to Lady Rodriguez Hospital at Peshawar. As the entire administration was in the hands of the army, it could not have been done without the army's assistance.

Malala was hit on the head, and it was clear to everybody, including the Pakistani army, that her life was in danger. So it was decided to carry her to the military hospital in Peshawar, away from Swat. About three at noon, the local army commander arrived at the hospital and informed that he was taking Malala and her father to Peshawar by an army helicopter.

The joint military hospital at Peshawar provides finest medical services to not only the army personnel but also their families. It was very tensed moments for Ziauddin. While he was ready to fly to Peshawar with his critically wounded daughter. His relatives had started to gather at his house for Malala's funeral.

On the other hand, Toorpekai did not have even this much time that she could assign her responsibility to someone and go with her daughter; therefore, it was decided to send Madam Mariam, the headmistress of the Kushhal Public School with them. Though Mariam's family was not in agreement with her going, as she had undergone a surgery a few days ago and she had a young child; yet Mariam considered Malala like her own daughter and she went with them.

The helipad was one kilometre away from the hospital, and the road was deserted. Ziauddin was afraid that the Taliban terrorists could strike the ambulance again; because the media had already declared who was inside the ambulance. Any way, they arrived at the helipad, and the helicopter arrived after a long wait, and in it boarded Malala, her father, her cousin Khanji, Ahmad Shah and Madam Mariam. None of them had ever before flown in a helicopter.

On the other hand, at Mingora, Malala's granny and Toorpekai's mother, was at her home. She urged the women present there to pray for Malala's well-being. She believed that God grants wishes to those having grey hair. Toorpekai was surprised to look at all of them. They all sat down on the mat and started to pray. Toorpekai said to those women: "Please don't make a noise, all of you pray for my daughter."

A little later, a man arrived at her door and giving a key said that he had found that key where Malala was shot. Toorpekai yelled at him: "I don't want the house key, I want my daughter."

When Malala's younger brothers heard of this shootout on television, they started crying. All this while, the telephone rang continuously; relatives called incessantly to know about the latest situation. Some of them opined that Malala must have died by then. This is not far to understand that all these things must have shaken the mother so badly, but she tried to maintain her balance and cool.

By this time, one of Ziauddin's friends rang up Toorpekai to inform that Malala was being flown to Peshawar as her condition was critical, and he advised her to go to Peshawar by road. The helipad was about one kilometre from the house too, so when it took to rotor and passed from above the house, Toorpekai climbed up the roof and praying for her well-being, flung her scarf into the air.

Malala was serious, she vomited blood in the helicopter too. Ziauddin was worried at the possible haemorrhage in the body.

After the helicopter landed at Peshawar, they thought that Malala would now be taken to the Lady Rodriguez Hospital, where Dr. Mumtaj, the well-known neurosurgeon was to take charge of her treatment, but she was taken to the Camberind Military Hospital, which was justifiable from security point of view.

Malala was shifted to the military hospital in an ambulance, where Colonel Zunaid Khan, a neurosurgeon, took over her charge. Ziauddin was unhappy to look at the doctor, because the colonel appeared neither a doctor nor a neurosurgeon. Looking at the confused Ziauddin, the colonel asked: "Is she your daughter?" Ziauddin shook his head in affirmative. He then examined Malala, stitched the wound above her eye where the bullet might have entered the body. He did not find the bullet in the CT scan that was taken at Mingora, so he was surprised, because there ought to be wound from where the bullet had gone out. He took a new CT scan and summoned Ziauddin.

The colonel said: "She was in senses in the beginning, but she was very restless and excited. Looking at her serious wound on the head, I have put her in the ICU. In four hours, I can see that her brain swelling has increased, causing her unconsciousness. The new scan reveals that the brain swelling is very serious because the bullet has passed through the brain, and it has damaged the brain bone. Although she needs the surgery to be done immediately but we cannot undertake it right now.

He further explained that a bone had broken, and its pieces had entered the brain causing increased swelling.

He then said: "I want to separate some part of the skull in order to house the swollen brain, else the pressure would become unbearable. This is inevitable to give her an opportunity to live. If we didn't do this, she might die, or she can suffer from paralysis, and I don't want this to happen to her."

Ziauddin could remember that the doctor at Mingora had said that it was a very ordinary wound, but here the colonel described it a very dangerous one. Just about this time, a friend advised if they could take Malala somewhere else.

Ziauddin was fully confused. He did not know what to do and what not to do. He expressed these sentiments to the colonel too. He said that it was no use keeping the girl there if she could not be treated immediately. At this, Dr. Zunaid got little annoyed: "If you think I cannot treat her, then I must tell you that such a patient is not new to me. I examine numerous cases of this type. I have undertaken thousands of surgeries. I examine and treat soldiers suffering from bullet wounds in the capacity of a neurosurgeon."

At this Ziauddin questioned himself and felt as it was wrong not to trust the doctor. A little later he said, "You are a doctor, do whatever you feel is correct. I am confused and not in a deciding mode" or not able to decide anything.

Towards the evening, Toorpekai arrived at Peshawar with Atal, her son and Mohammad Farukh (Ziauddin's friend). Madam Mariam advised her not to cry or weep at seeing Malala, because she could listen and understand everything. Ziauddin asked her to be ready to confront any news as worst as worst could be. She was completely shaken. When she visited Malala in the ward, her eyes were moist and voice deep. She had to try hard to say a few words: "Malala, Atal has come to see you."

Atal could not control himself, he broke out crying. A hospital attendant came there and took him to the place in the hospital where they were to stay.

At midnight, Dr. Zunaid informed Ziauddin that the brain swelling was continuously increasing and she had vomited blood again, and there was no other way but to undertake the surgery. Ziauddin was unnerved at this. He said: "Will she survive?"

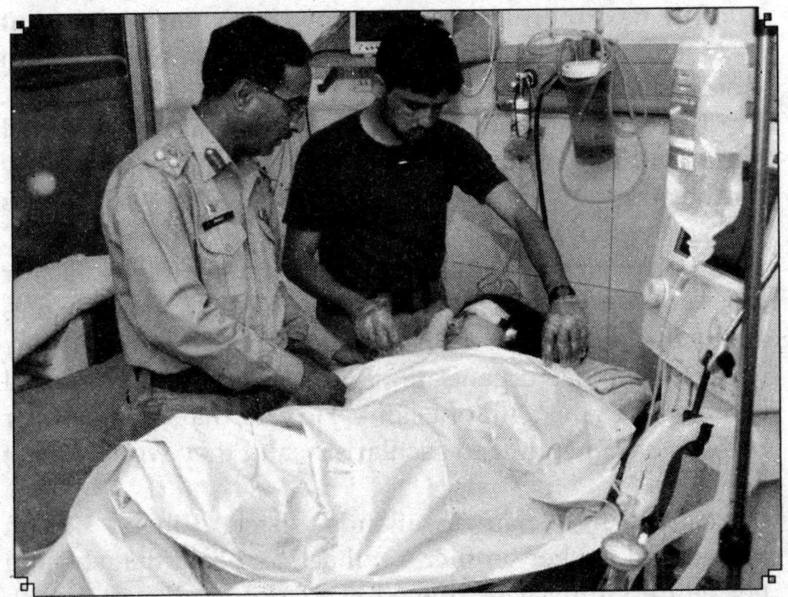

Dr. Zunaid assured him mildly, and also informed him that Dr. Mumtaz too was about to reach there to help him. Listening to this, he immediately concurred for the surgery. To prepare for the procedure, her long beautiful hair was shaved off. The surgery started at half past one at night. The skull bone was cut off and kept in her belly for safe-keeping, which had to be reconnected to the brain later. Blood clots and damaged tissues were removed from the brain. This took five hours, while Ziauddin walked up and down the corridor. Suddenly, a nurse ran out of the operation theatre towards him Ziauddin thought that all was lost. She was sure to bring some bad news, but she asked him to run to the blood bank as Malala needed blood urgently. This assured him. He thanked God that she was still alive. Dr. Zunaid walked out of the theatre after five and a half hours, when Ziauddin asked him politely: "Doctor, I know this is a stupid question, still I ask it. Will she survive?"

"In my profession, two and two don't always make four, Mr. Ziauddin. We have done our work and now you have to wait for the outcome."

The next morning brought good news for Malala, but the doctors thought it fit to keep her in coma, else her brain would have to resume working.

In the meanwhile, news filtered in that the banned outfit Tehrik-e-Taliban Pakistan took over the responsibility for the attack. Its spokesman Ahsanullah Ahsan said: "This girl was criticizing *jihad* and Taliban, so she was attacked. This is a warning to all those who try to follow her or raise voice against us. We had Warned her several times about this, and had told her to stop cooperating with the non-government organisations of western countries, and come back to the path of Islam." He said that they shot her because she encouraged secularism, and they would target her again.

Surprisingly, an assailant's sister, Rihana Halim apologized for her brother's evil act, and said that she and her entire family was grieved at this cowardly act, which has brought shame to them.

Rihana Halim, sister of 23-year-old terrorist Ataullah Khan described the activities of her brother and said to convey to Malala that she begged sorry for her brother's act. She said: "He has brought shame on our entire family. He has robbed us of our honour; it is an unbearable act."

Expressing her grief at this, Rihana said that Malala was like her sister and expressed solidarity with her. She hoped that she would recover soon and live a happy and normal life in the times to come. Praying to God, she hoped that Malala would not accept her or her family as the enemy. She severed all connections with Ataullah, her brother.

The police officers claimed that they were looking for Khan and two others who had shot 15-year-old Malala. They said that Ataullah Khan was a physics graduate from the Jehanjeb College, and the plan for attack on her had been made in Afghanistan. This assailant had been caught in 2009 during a military operation but he had been set free three months later.

But this time, more than 50 Imams linked with the Sunni Ittehad Council in Pakistan issued a *fatwa* regarding shootout at Malala and condemned this attack as non-Islamic. Hamid Syed Qazmi, former minister of religious matters, supported these Imams, who appealed for displaying solidarity with Malala. They said in the *fatwa:* "The Islam does not forbid women from taking education. The assailants have violated the Islamic edicts."

The same evening, Amir Ahmad Khan, chief of the Urdu service of the BBC, in an interview to the *Time* magazine, expressed regret at the incident with Malala and said: "Today I think sitting at my desk that it would not have happened had we not found her out. It does never mean that I don't appreciate her contribution; I express confidence in children like Malala who firmly believe in what they are doing."

Madonna, the popular pop star, dedicated a special song to Malala. Singing the Human Nature's song, she said that this was a song praying for Malala's well-being. She said: "Support education, support women." She said that this dastardly act had made her cry. In the same sense, Adam B. Ellick, *New York Times* journalist, who had made a documentary on her, said: "My little video star is fighting for life."

Colonel Zunaid had only heard about Malala, but had never met her before, but he knew that she was some distinguished personality because the Pakistani media thronged the hospital compound, and communicated her minute-to-minute condition to the people.

Speaking about this, Hamid Mir, a television presenter, said: "This assault has made the country feel that the Taliban is capable of shooting a young girl, though she retains enough courage and vigour to speak against the enemies; if they can target that little girl, they can target anybody."

Malala gradually recovered in the ICU at Peshawar. The progress of her health was a talking point not only in Pakistan, but also in the whole world. General Ashfaq Kiyani, Chief of Staff took interest in this matter and wanted a definite and independent advice in the matter. He visited the hospital a few hours after the surgery. He said: "The entire country is praying for you and your daughter." Ziauddin knew General Ashfaq from 2009 when he had visited Swat after the defeat of the Taliban. At that occasion, Malala had expressed her joy that he had done a fine thing to expel the Taliban from there, and now what was needed was only to arrest Fazlullah. These words from her filled the hall with a loud sound of clapping. At that time, General Kiyani had tapped her head in affection.

Dr. Zunaid apprised General Kiyani about Malala in detail, and told him about the future course of treatment too. At this, General Kiyani advised that the CT scan might be sent abroad for specialist's advice.

After this visit, Malala's security was further strengthened. Nobody was allowed to see her. Her condition improved somewhat, which made everybody hopeful that she could be saved now.

In Britain, a young Muslim leader Mariam Hual said: "Malala is a source of inspiration for people, my own sister has been influenced by her, and now she has realized the significance of education, else she always evaded books."

Ziauddin was worried about Malala's health, and he continuously prayed God for her complete recovery. God seemed to have granted his wish too. It was a mere coincidence that a team of British doctors from Birmingham, on General Kiyani's invitation, was on a visit to Pakistani army to advise about liver transplant procedures. This team was being led by Javed Kiyani, an emergency care advisor. He was a British Pakistani, who continued to maintain relations with his place of birth. He was working in the Elizabeth Hospital in Birmingham. The General had instructed this team to see him before leaving in order to apprise him of the progress of their programme. Just on the following day, two doctors of the team called on General Kiyani's residence. At this time, the television was broadcasting a programme on Malala. The General said to Dr. Zunaid: "It would be better that you examined Malala before leaving for Britain."

Dr. Zunaid immediately concurred, and the General talked to his officers regarding this.

When this request reached Javed Kiyani, he knew well who all comprised his team and who could go to Peshawar with him. His clear choice was for Fiona Reynolds, a child intensive care specialist, though she was somewhat reserved about her security there. She knew about the risk of visiting the place from the newspaper reports. However, when she came to know that she had to examine the same Malala who had started the campaign for poor girls' education, she nodded in affirmative and said: "Malala, as a girl, wanted to get education, but she was shot just for this, while I am an educated woman and am fortunately in Pakistan, so I must go there."

After Dr. Kiyani assured her of security, Fiona got ready to go to Peshawar.

The army hospital doctors did not like this visit, but when they were told on whose invitation it was visiting, they allowed the team to examine Malala. The doctors did not find her condition satisfactory. According to Reynolds, the surgery was done at the right time and it had been done well, but the after-care was not as perfect as it ought to be. Comparing such a patient in Britain, Fiona said: "Such a patient in Britain is kept under continuous watch through an arterial line, but according to her chart, her blood pressure was taken two hours ago."

This made Ziauddin happy. Now he felt that Malala was in the right hands. Dark was setting in, Dr. Javed gave up his intention to leave for Rawalpindi. The team left for Islamabad the next day, Wednesday, as thev were scheduled to leave for Birmingham on Thursday.

Reynolds's inner-self kept saying that Malala could be saved if she was given due care at the right time. She knew it well that only intensive care could bring desirable results. There were more possibilities of her brain functions recovering keeping in mind the capability of the patient's willpower for struggle.

The same day, Ziauddin was given Malala's passport by the internal security minister, which indicated that Malala could be sent abroad for treatment. It was a burdensome evening for him and his wife because the passport meant taking Malala abroad or to heaven. The same day, he asked his brother to prepare for her funeral. He was mentally prepared for her death; however, Toorpekai was not at all ready to think God could summon Malala at so young age.

When General Kiyani received the medical report by Dr. Javed and Dr. Fiona about hospital and Malala, he sent two military doctors from Islamabad to Peshawar. Those two doctors observed that the attitude was a relaxed one as far as the treatment was concerned. One of these two doctors, Brigadier Aslam informed Dr. Fiona that Malala's condition was turning worse, her blood pressure was going down, the kidney was under danger as urine did not pass, while blood acid and sugar levels shot up. It appeared as if all efforts were going to prove futile.

Dr. Fiona had already arrived at the airport for her flight to Birmingham. Her luggage had been booked in, but when she was informed about Malala's worsening condition, she decided to help her. She had two nurses of the Birmingham Hospital with her too. She postponed her flight and decided to go to Peshawar immediately. When she reached Malala, she was much worried at her falling health, it appeared as if her kidney was about to fail, while her heart and blood circulation seemed to stop functioning; and urgent medication was needed to aid unstable blood pressure. Reynolds thought if she could live, but there were few chances of getting better neurologic results, as her condition was very poor. In such a case, any brain damage could lead to an irrecoverable situation.

Soon, she said to Ziauddin, "Mr. Ziauddin, Malala will have to be shifted to Rawalpindi military hospital where there is better equipped intensive care unit."

"But, Dr. Fiona, my child is very serious, how can she be shifted in this condition?"

"You need not worry, I'll go with her, I have done such things before," she assured Ziauddin.

"Are there any hopes of her surviving?"

"Had I no hopes, I wouldn't have been here, I would have been in Birmingham now," said she.

Ziauddin's eyes streamed down. Just then, a nurse administered an eye drop to Malala. Seeing this, Toorpekai said: "Did you see that? Dr. Fiona is right, had she no hope, the nurse wouldn't have given her the eye drop."

Malala was flown by helicopter to Rawalpindi in the care of Dr. Fiona. Ziauddin noticed that she kept an alert watch on all the machines in the flight extending over one hour and a quarter. Finding her busy all the time, Ziauddin asked her: "Do you keep so busy in Birmingham too?"

"Yes, of course, I look after complicated cases there, but this is the first case of this type. Besides, it is also connected with British honour."

"How do you say that?"

"I am aware that the white are not appreciated in Pakistan. If something were to happen to Malala, people would take no time to accuse that a white woman has killed her; moreover, her death would simply mean the death of Pakistan's Mother Teresa.

"Oh, is this the reason that you are taking her there?"

"Yes, and if needed, I would take her to Birmingham too. My Birmingham nurses will look after at the Armed Forces Institute of Cardiology Hospital at Rawalpindi," said Dr. Fiona with a smile.

Under Fiona's care, Malala's condition stabilized over the next two days. However, the danger persisted if high quality care was not given in the next 48 to 72 hours, so Reynolds enquired about her resettlement. In fact, this case pertained to the honour of Pakistan. Reynolds advised: "If Pakistani army and government want better outcomes, all those facilities would be needed here which are available in many countries outside Pakistan."

At this, General Kiyani talked to Dr. Javed and Dr. Fiona for six hours, which is an important thing for such a high officer to do. General Kiyani did not want Malala to die, and he was looking for the best possible treatment. Dr. Javed recommended the names of several well-known hospitals in Edinburg, Glasgow and Britain. Finally, the General said: "Why don't you take her to your own hospital? I know that wounded Afghan and Iraqi troops are treated there; moreover, your hospital is renowned for its facilities."

Dr. Javed was astonished to listen to this from the chief of Pakistan army. Immediately, he talked to the main officer in his hospital at Birmingham. He received immediate concurrence from him.

Now the problem revolved round how to shift Malala to Birmingham. Dr. Javed advised General Kiyani: "The Afghan Royal Air Force could be contacted for help as it transports wounded troops from Afghanistan."

"No, we can't trust them, as they are infamous as CIA agents. If Malala suffered something untoward in their aircraft, it would bring great turmoil here. So, we would not use their aircraft for her," the General opined seriously.

"What is the way out then?"

"Let us see, some way will have to be found out. Moreover, the British Government is ready to help, but it needs an official request, which should take some time to get."

"General, I entreat you to ensure that it should not take too much time to endanger Malala either," said Dr. Fiona in an anxious tone.

About this time, the General got information that the royal family of the UAE had offered to give its private jet which was equipped with all necessary medical facilities.

"Look, I said that some way would be found out," said the General happily. "I have already seen to it that the Pakistani Government would pay for all the expenses on her treatment."

"You have done a fine thing. It would greatly relieve the Yousafzai family."

While the family was happy with this facility, it faced another problem; that was, only Ziauddin could travel with Malala to Britain as no other family member had a passport. Other members could not be sent immediately as they lacked passports and visas. When a colonel informed of this, Faiz Mohammad, Malala's uncle, was standing there. He said to Ziauddin: "This lonely woman may have to suffer behind you."

Ziauddin was undecided. On the one hand, he had to decide upon their journey for his daughter's treatment abroad and any delay could aggravate her condition; and on the other, it involved a great risk to leave behind his wife and two sons at the place where Malala had been shot at. Finally, he said to the colonel that he could not go leaving behind his wife and two sons and that he was ready to send Malala alone. It surprised Dr. Javed greatly, he took him aside and asked: "Is it true what you are saying, or is there something else behind this decision?"

Ziauddin said: "My wife has asked me not to leave her alone."

Dr. Javed placed his hand on his shoulder and said: "Well, Ziauddin brother, if it is so, we'll take care of Malala in the best way we can. Will you have trust in us?"

"I have complete faith in you. I know that God Himself has sent you to me like his angels. It is no less than a miracle for you to visit us after the disaster."

"Ziauddin brother, it is God who sends a solution before He sends a problem; don't you think so?" Ziauddin nodded his head to concur with him.

Ziauddin signed all the papers designating Dr. Fiona as Malala's guardian in Britain. Before leaving, he folded hands before her and said: "Please, doctor, take care of my daughter."

When Ziauddin and his wife came near Malala's bed to bid her farewell, they found her lying with closed eyes, they could perceive her breath, which declared to them that she was alive. It was about eleven at night. Toorpekai could not control herself on seeing the affectionate daughter; her patience flowed away in the forms of tears, while Ziauddin controlled himself somehow. He could not have cried, it only would have weakened Toorpekai. By this time, the critical period of 72 hours had past; with this, Malala's condition was better than before with less swelling and improved blood level. The parents now believed that the British doctors would do everything right.

Not long after, when Ziauddin and his family were in the hostel room, there was a knock at the door. Anxious, he answered the call promptly, and found at the door the same colonel who had been sent by the General earlier too.

On entering inside, he asked Ziauddin to accompany Malala to Britain, which angered him. He said in a strict tone: "You are troubling me unnecessarily. I have decided what I wanted to. I have signed all the papers too." At this, the other officer accompanying the colonel said: "You must accompany your daughter. She is yet a child, due to which she would not be admitted to the British hospital, and all our hard work would be rendered meaningless."

"Look," said Ziauddin, "I suppose destiny is bound to happen. I cannot change my decision. In a few days, our papers will be ready, and then we all will go to Britain."

They argued for a while, and then the army officer said: "Well, don't go if you don't wish to, but you will have to come over with us to sign some papers in the hospital." All these papers belonged to permission for keeping an eye over his family; the officers made him sign them.

Early in the morning, Malala was taken to the Rawalpindi airport under military watch. All roads leading to the airport were sealed. The UAE aircraft was like a miniature hospital, equipped with all required emergency appliances. It flew via Abu Dhabi to Birmingham.

While the aircraft took Malala away, there were news stories that the Taliban had now threatened her father. Owing to this threat, the number of girls in the school diminished. When this news broke out in *The News*, guardians and girls felt threatened, the school administration too confirmed that the institution had been threatened.

Principal Mariam of the Kushhal Public School confirmed that a threat had been received. Looking at its security, the administration forbade the school students from talking to the media. It had a clear impact. The number of girls attending school fell down drastically, while some girls sought admission in other schools, others were scared of the media coverage. This was the reason that the school administration did not allow the students to talk to the media. The school administrator, Iqbal Hussain, said that the school's prestige was being adversely affected.

Ziauddin too instructed the administration not to allow the media to interfere in the school matters and enter the classes because it harmed studies.

At that time, there was a flood of status reports on the Facebook and Twitter, like:

"The CIA is behind attack on Malala."

"Malala is a CIA agent."

Most of these remarks came from the middle and educated class of Pakistan. Some of them wrote: "This is a bid to bring a bad name to Pakistan and Taliban."

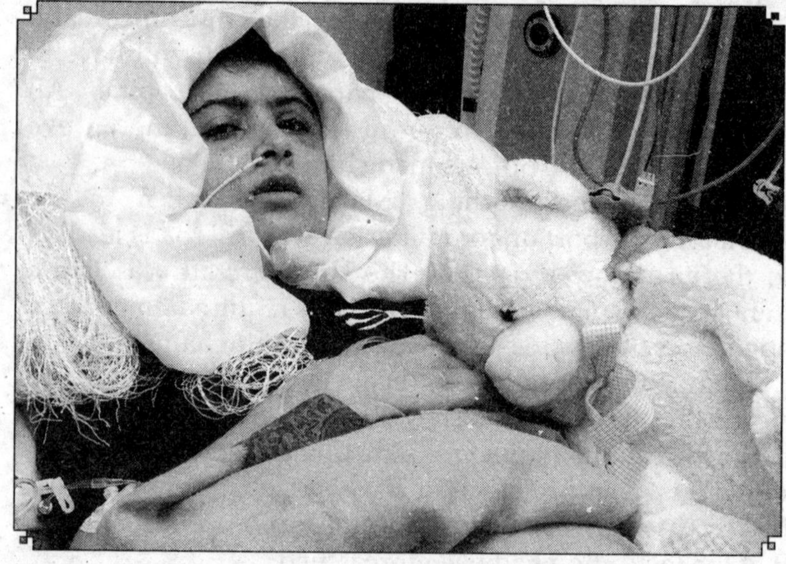

The liberal analysts in Pakistan viewed that Pakistani people liked the theory of conspiracy. They said that it is very common and easy to hold the West responsible for any ill that might occur in a country whose economy is devastated, where inflation and unemployment are at the topmost level, where a corrupt government rules and where electricity cuts and suicide attacks are the order of the day. A comment on the Facebook claimed that Malala was attacked so that the people of Pakistan might stop opposing the film called *The Innocence of Muslim*.

Some people posted some photographs on the Internet after trickery on the Photoshop, in which Malala and her father had been shown with some American officers. Besides, a photograph of dead children too was shown claiming that they all had died in drone attacks. The photograph had a caption: Don't they need any sympathy?

In yet another Facebook post, Barack Obama, President of US, was shown laughing with some officers, and it carried a caption: Sir, they still think that the Taliban has attacked Malala.

A Karachi-based analyst, Mansur Raza said that the people having sympathy with the Taliban and fundamentalist religious organisations were spreading rumours to mislead people. He said: "A bid is being made to reduce the significance of this attack because most of the Pakistanis have condemned this attack."

Hamid Satti, an Islamabad-based psychologist, said: "In my opinion, this is being done so as to hold somebody else responsible. In place of facing bitter truth, we try to blame others. This is the way of defending ourselves."

A Karachi student condemned attack on Malala and said: "The Pakistanis hate Americans, but at the same time, are influenced by it too. They think that America is having some divine power. They think that it can do anything, it can make people disappear, bring flood, drop something from the sky."

While all these comments were being posted, the truth remained that these very people could go to any extent to get an American visa. The human rights organisations condemned the attack on Malala and favoured education for girls. Zahida Hina, a Pakistani writer, said: "The Taliban is barbaric and does not believe in humanity. The 14-year-old Malala became a threat for the Taliban only because she was worth emulating by other girls. The Taliban has attacked her because it wanted to tell that the other girls following in her shoes would meet the same fate."

Ziauddin negated those news stories which claimed that he might seek asylum abroad. He said: "I can only laugh at it first, as the goal of all our sacrifices, including attack on my daughter, could not be so trivial to migrate to some other country and live their all life."

□

7

Malala in Unknown City

On 15 October 2012, Malala was shifted to the Queen Elizabeth Hospital in Birmingham for the next three months. She was kept under medical observation and care so she cames out of the coma but later, during the day, they decided to bring Malala out of the coma the very next day. The last piece of memory Malala had was of the ill-fated bus journey. Now, when she opened her eyes, she found herself surrounded by strangers in a foreign country. On 16 October, when she opened her eyes, the first thing that she thought was: "Thanks Heavens, I am not yet dead." She could perceive that she was not in her country, but she did not know where exactly she was.

She felt a severe headache, even the injection could not control it. Her left ear bled, and she could feel that the left side of the face did not function well. She gazed at the nurse standing away; she felt her eyes watery, she was unable to hear with the left ear, nor was she able to move her jaw.

Malala's parents and brothers were yet in Pakistan, but Dr. Javed Kiyani stood near her head. On gaining senses, she found all the strangers there, she was scared a little. Recalling this moment, Dr. Kiyani said: "When she came out of the coma, she appeared very scared; her eyes revealed that she was trying to recall the past events, and she was trembling with the fear that something untoward had occurred to her father.

We knew that she could not speak because a tube had been inserted under the throat to allow her to breathe, but I knew that she could hear, so I told her who I was and where she was. She moved her eyes to tell that she now understood it."

Malala wished to write, so pad and pencil were brought. She tried to write, but could not grip pencil; it was due to the injury on the head. Then, an alphabet board was brought, and then she pointed to different letters to tell what she wanted to.

The first word she asked in this way was 'country', Dr. Kiyani said that she was in England. The next word was 'father', and she was informed that he was in Pakistan and would come over in a few days. This was all they talked that day.

The people allowed for 'more talks' included Dr. Fiona Reynolds, who brought a pink notebook for Malala, in which she could write her questions. Reynolds said that she started writing in that notebook, which immensely relaxed her, and the doctors heaved a sigh of relief when they saw her questioning.

Dr. Kiyani and Dr. Fiona were happy to find positive improvement in Malala. Expressing fears, Fiona said: "I wish that she has not lost her cognitive abilities."

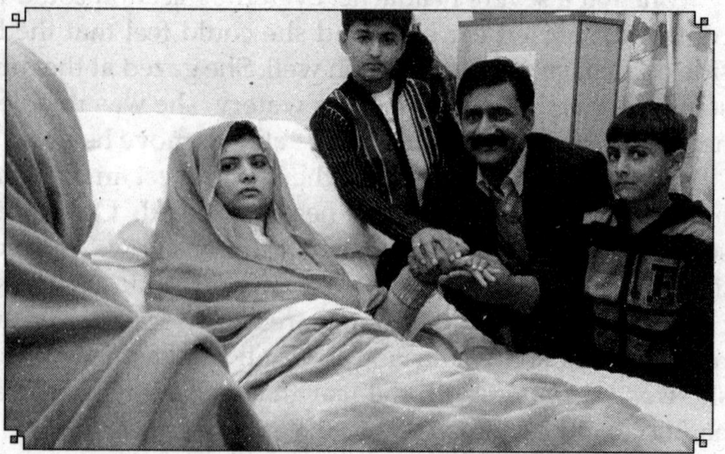

Dr. Kiyani said: "I hoped that her speech ability would not get affected by the head injury and it is wonderful that nothing of that sort happened."

"Rather she is talking to us in the third language, which means that she still remembers her mother tongue Pashto, second language Urdu as well as English."

"Yes, Fiona, the part of the brain linked with language, speech and cognition is intact."

Malala recovered wonderfully. It was not only owing to the doctors' care and treatment, but also her own willpower for life, which inspired her to overcome such a terrible shock.

The day she came out of the intensive care, her parents had already reached Birmingham, and they were brought to the hospital on that day. It was 26th October. Malala was curiously waiting to meet her family members. Sixteen days ago she had parted with her mother to go to school, ever since she had changed four hospitals and travelled thousands of kilometres. These sixteen days were like sixteen years. The hospital staff shifted her from the ICU to the general ward. Dr. Javed got her bed set so that he could welcome her family members.

Ziauddin and Toorpekai too were restless, so as soon as they were called, they hurried to her room calling her name. Toorpekai kissed her hand and took her in arms. She had not cried all these days in hospital despite being alone, but that day she cried aloud, as if the contained tempest had burst out with a flood of tears. They all wept for a while, and then they were able to control themselves. Her parents found that her left eye was infirm and the face had bent aside, she was weak by the left ear. They kept their patience even on noticing all these things. They pointed out to the road outside the hospital. Malala could look at England for the first time. Unconsciously, she started to compare England with Pakistan, and she felt there was a divide poles apart between the two places located on the same earth.

Malala felt that her parents were very upset, but they tried to conceal their emotions, while her father felt that his daughter was unable to smile being unable to move her jaw.

Ziauddin was very proud of his daughter's unforgettable smile and giggle, but that day, he softly said to Toorpekai: "We have lost smile and laughter from her glorious shining face. The Taliban is very cruel, it has snatched away smile from our child."

When Ziauddin walked out of the room, the media surrounded him. He was unable to say anything, as if his voice had been vanquished. He gathered his confidence and said in a trembling voice: "Malala is better now, and God willing, she would once again play and study. She was unconscious when she flew off from Pakistan, but now I find her conscious, and this gives me confidence that she would recover fully."

Malala was getting cards from the country and abroad wishing her 'Get well soon'. It was all the result of people's prayers and good wishes that she recovered from the coma. Asif Ali Zardari, President of Pakistan, himself visited Birmingham to see her. Not only this, he also signed that appeal in which millions of people had appealed for donation for poor families for sending daughters to school. This appeal was meant to honour Malala.

The paralysis on left side of the face became a challenge for the doctors. It was a great problem for her parents too. They were actively thinking what all could be done about this. Later, sharing his experiences of this time, Ziauddin said once: "At that time, when she tried to smile, I used to turn to my wife and try to read her emotions; she seemed to say that it was not our Malala who she had given birth to; it was the girl who had enlivened our lives."

According to the neurosurgeon Dr. Richard Irving, who treated her. "She was quite perplexed at the change of her face in the beginning. He said: "She was unwilling to speak at the initial stages and liked to be photographed from the side not affected by paralysis. It was a sentimental impact, which she could not divulge to anyone, but it is quite simple to understand a 15-year-old girl like her."

After tests and scans, Irving opined and announced that nerves of the face could not be hoped to recover and moreover the status of the nervous system cannot be judged until surgery is done. The problem was the surgery was a lengthy procedure and Malala's body was not in a condition to endure the risk in the operation.

But she was in control of herself. It was seen that she discussed with her father, but she took her decisions herself. She took deep interest in her treatment, as if she did not want to leave it to anybody.

Ziauddin felt guilty on seeing his delicate daughter in this condition. One day, he asked Toorpekai who was really disturbed about her face: "Tell me the truth, do you think I am responsible for all that happened with Malala?"

Toorpekai said: "No, Not at all. Forget about all this. You didn't send Malala for theft, murder or any crime, rather, you and Malala were trying to execute good deeds. Why should you hold yourself guilty?

Ziauddin thought that it was he who had led Malala to writing blogs. At that time, he had not dreamed that this could happen to her because when the Taliban had destroyed hundreds of schools, even then they had not harmed even a child or teacher. How then could they attack Malala?

In fact, both Ziauddin and Toorpekai were desperate at her suffering. Malala knew this, so she often hid her suffering. The Yousafzai family had been in Birmingham just for four days, while high officials from three countries had already visited her. They included Rehman Malik, internal security minister of Pakistan; William Hughes, British foreign minister; and Sheikh Abdullah bin Jayed, UAE foreign minister. The hospital administration informed about this to the Yousafzai family but did not allow them to meet Malala, as they wanted Malala to recover fully. Rehman Malik told Ziauddin to convey to Malala that she should smile for the sake of the nation. Ziauddin did not say a word. He thought had he been capable to do so, he would have rather already done it. Rehman Malik also informed him that the Pakistani Government had announced a reward of one lakh dollars on Ataullah Khan, Malala's assailant. He was sure that he would be apprehended one day.

Ziauddin said that only two people had been caught ever since the assault. One was Usman the van driver and the other, accountant of his school because he had rung up Usman soon after the assault to know about the incident. This reveals that neither of them is involved in the case, why had they been arrested then? This was beyond any logic. If it was Ataullah Khan who attacked then it was he who must be arrested.

On 15 October, Gordon Brown, former Prime Minister of Britain, filed a petition in her name; he gave the call 'I am Malala'. The main demand in the petition was that there should not be any child who would not go to school by 2015. Malala will go to school soon, she remains a true inspiration for girls' education the world over. She is a shining, glorious, resplendent star. He admired her courage and determination. He said that he was sure she would emerge as a true leader to send every boy and every girl to school. In November 2012, when Brown visited Islamabad, he handed over this petition to President Asif Ali Zardari.

On the other hand, the UN announced that 10 November would be observed as Malala Day the world over, the very next day, Malala was scheduled to undergo facial surgery; and the doctor was, Neurosurgeon Richard Irving.

During the ten-hour-long surgery, Irving noted that her nerves had been severed owing to the bullet; the two ends of the nerves were linked, but as two-centimetre-long part could not be found, the nerves did not resume their original form, due to which he decided to shorten the nervous path.

Malala had to wait for three months after this surgery to start using this part. Gradually, the left side started to function. She did all the exercises that the doctors recommended. A few days later, she recovered from the terrible headache which had persisted. Now she loved to read her favourite books. Seeing this, Ziauddin and Toorpekai were confident that she would be able to recover her memory completely. One month later, she was permitted to step out of the hospital.

In December 2012, Pakistan and the UNESCO signed an agreement to establish a fund for encouragement and aid to girls' education in Pakistan and other countries. This was named as Malala Fund. This agreement was signed by Sheikh Wakas Akram, Pakistan's education minister and Irene Bokova, director of the UNESCO, at the UN headquarters in Paris. On this occasion, President Asif Ali Zardari too was present. Later in April 2013, Malala announced release of the first installment of 45,000 dollars from Malala Fund to an organisation located in the Swat valley in Pakistan. With this, Angelina Jolly, a Hollywood actress and special ambassador of the UN, promised to donate 2,00,000 dollars to the Fund. This organisation has promised to provide uniforms, books and other teaching materials to the girls together with their admission to schools.

□

8
Beginning of a New Life

On a pleasant December morning, Malala was sent to the Birmingham Botanical Garden with Toorpekai. Ziauddin did not accompany her in order to keep the media away. Malala was very happy that day because she was going to see any other country than Pakistan for the first time in her life. She objected to her being seated in the middle seat, she wanted to sit near the window and enjoy the outside scenery. She was being seated in the middle lest her head should strike against window or ceiling; when this fact was revealed to her, she happily took the middle seat. Not only Malala was extremely happy to see the natural scenery that spread far and wide before her eyes, but her mother was also happy to see her daughter recovering quickly. On return from the garden, Toorpekai said to Ziauddin: "It's for the first time that I am happy."

The Yousafzai family already knew that President Asif Ali Zardari was about to visit them. He was scheduled to come on 8 December. The hospital administration did not want him to visit the hospital, as the media could crowd the premises, but it was not possible for Ziauddin to prevent this visit from the head of the nation who had agreed to pay a sum of two lakh pounds for Malala's treatment. Above all this, the Yousafzai family had been given a rented apartment in the middle of Birmingham town. It was their duty to welcome the guest.

When the President arrived at hospital with his daughter, barely one year older than Malala, the media thronged the hospital. He was welcomed by Dr. Fiona. After he talked about her health, he handed over the bouquet and said to Ziauddin: "You people are fortunate that you could bring her to Britain for treatment. Had she lived in Pakistan, I doubt if she could have recovered fully. "Now she will have her smile back."

The President was accompanied by the Pakistani High Commissioner in London. The President said to him: "Let Mr. Ziauddin be appointed in the education attaché in Britain itself, and he should be given a good salary so that he can survive here." Ziauddin informed him that Gordon Brown, former Prime Minister and UN envoy, had proposed him to become an honorary advisor. The President said: "No problem, you can take up both the jobs."

Ziauddin Yousafzai was appointed the special advisor of the UN for world education on 10 December, 2012. He named the plan for sending all children to school by 2015 as Malala Plan. Ziauddin was appointed to assist in this plan.

On the occasion when the UN appointed him the special ambassador for global education programme, he delivered a speech, which is worth knowing for any father. He said:

> "My name is Ziauddin Yousafzai. I am the father of a brave daughter, Malala. In our paternalistic community, a father is known by the name of his son, but here I am who is known by the name of his daughter, and it is a matter of pride for me. Those days, when Pakistan was eclipsed under the shadow of the Taliban, girls were forbidden from studying, Malala continued with her education. Not only this, she motivated other girls to continue to get education. During that period, the people of the BBC contacted me. They wanted that one of the children, that I taught, should write a column for the BBC, but none of the parents agreed for this. All of them were terrified of the Taliban and then Malala came forward. Despite all the dangers involved, she took up

the pen to describe the suffering that the girls in Swat underwent. She was only twelve years old then. She started a campaign for girls' education and rights, and gradually she became popular among people. Then she became a well-known name all over the world. There is much difference between then and now. She used to be my daughter then, but today, I am her father. She is popular the world over, people don't know her as my daughter, rather they know me as her father.

"In our society, especially in rural areas, no celebration is held when daughters are born. Birth of a daughter is considered as good as a shameful and sorrowful occurrence. When daughters grow up, they are told to keep within their limits. But nothing of the sort happened in our family. We celebrated Malala's birth joyfully. After her birth, I entered her name in our family tree register, in which only sons' names were entered. This register is as old as three hundred years. When Malala grew up, we got her admitted to school, not to get education, but to identify herself as an independent individual. Quite contrary to the orthodox thinking of my community, I explained to my daughter that there was no need to be limited within the 'so-called limit'.

"There are a lot of dreaded customs when it comes to daughters. You will find few inspiring instances related to women. Being a woman simply means a victim of violence, discrimination and exploitation. An individual who must bear with injustice without expressing a word. A person does not welcome a daughter at her birth. When she is five years old, she is hidden away in place of sending her to school. When she is thirteen years old, she is restricted within the four walls of the house. She cannot step out without a male member accompanying her. When she grows up, she becomes an object of honour for her father, brother and family. In the name of this so-called limitation, a scope is defined, within which she is forced to follow a specific code of conduct. If a girl tried to step out of this scope, she would simply be killed.

"If we wished, we could change the lives of our daughters. We can bring out women out of the suffering they are facing all over the world. It entails that all men and women should break barriers of orthodox thinking. We will have to destroy some old rules to change the situation, the rules which advocate discrimination against women. We will have to show courage. The twenty-first century belongs to women. We will have to look at women's rights as human rights. Women must be identified as independent individuals now.

"Malala has been struggling for education right since her childhood. She has raised her voice from all available forums. We are happy that her voice was heard all over the world. Malala was not terrified of anybody. The Taliban assaulted her, this assault took place at a time when she was returning home after her examination by school van. In fact, the Taliban is not scared of bombs, but books and pens. Malala was shot in the head, which means brain. Maybe they want to aim at women's brains. They don't want daughters to live freely in our country. My daughter has fought a very tough battle. She did not bow down before all these powers. She knows how to control herself in a difficult situation. I am happy that the world has stood by her side in this fight.

"People often ask me if I have trained my daughter, how she became so daring. I only say, don't ask what I have done, rather ask what I haven't done. I have not clipped her wings, I have not blocked her path, I didn't ask her to live within the orthodox scope. I encouraged her, I motivated her. I allowed her to do everything that she wanted to do. Friends! trust your daughters, they are worth your trust. Give them education, they are the masters of fantastic capabilities. Give them respect which they fully deserve."

With the onset of 2013, Malala's life started to witness those changes which dawn in the life of achievers. In the last week of January, two American senators presented a bill in the name of peace worker Malala Yousafzai, which provided for scholarship to Pakistani girls. This bill was brought by Barbara Boxer and Mary Landrew. It was aimed to provide educational opportunities to the girls lacking facilities in Pakistan. This made Malala's destination towards education a step nearer. It was also decided that there will be a provision of thirty percent increase in scholarships over the next four years. These additional scholarships were to go to women.

Presenting the bill, Barbara said: "Malala Yousafzai has very courageously supported girls' education. Education should be a basic right for girls and women. This bill is not only to recognize Malala's unique courage, but also to ensure that more girls in Pakistan are able to realize their dreams through higher education."

Malala has already received for the Nobel Prize, for which Malala undertook a videoconference with Ban Ki Moon, General Secretary of the UN. This video was watched the world over how Malala had expressed her resolve to play the role of a leader in service of the world. Ban Ki Moon described her a symbol of hope, and said that Malala, who was targeted by the Taliban on the issue of girls' education, is a symbol of hope and a daughter of the UN.

In the same video, Ban said to Malala: "The UN stands behind you and scores of people like you, for everybody knows that when we educate a woman, we educate a family, a community and a country."

Having risen as a symbol of the country's struggle against the Taliban, this Pakistani adolescent was honoured with the bravery award by the World Peace and Prosperity Foundation for her bravery and raising her voice for women's education under adverse circumstances prevailing in Swat. This award was given to her on 19 November 2012.

This award was given by Prince Ali Khan, the chairman of this foundation in the House of Lords. This award was received by S. Zulfikar Gardeji, Deputy High Commissioner of Pakistan in Britain, on her behalf.

On 9 January 2013, Malala was given the French award Simone de Beauvoir, for her campaign in the cause of girls' education. This award was received by her father on her behalf.

In February 2013, she underwent another surgery under which a titanium plate was inserted at the place where a part of the skull. Pakistani surgeons had removed a part of the skull. An ear prosthesis was also inserted in her left ear. She was assured that she didn't need any more surgeries then. Her face continued to recover with physiotherapy.

And then the day came when, after her recovery, she went to school in Britain for the first time. It was 21 March 2013, she was registered in the Edgbaston High School in Birmingham. Malala set out on her new voyage of life with a pink schoolbag on her shoulders and a black scarf on her head. She termed the first day at school as the most important day of her life. This 15-year-old girl said: "I am pleased that my dream to go to school again has been realized. I have books, I will study in school, and I want that every girl in the world gets this opportunity. Of course, I am missing my classmates of Pakistan."

Starting from the ninth grade, Malala expressed her desire to study politics and law in future. The Edgbaston High School is one of the oldest schools in Britain, and Pakistan government is paying about 8.17 lakh rupees as her annual fee. Dr. Ruth, school Principal, said: "Malala wishes to live like an ordinary adolescent. She wants that her new companions should cooperate with her. I talked to her and found that she missed her school while in the hospital."

Malala is missing her lost friends, but she knows that life means to move on. Whatever she has attained, could have been done by none else but her, and all this might not be repeated, as it was a strange phenomenon. Malala's words are those magic nectar which find their way right inside the heart. This girl has suffered much to attain this moral force.

It was decided to honour Malala with the 'Dutch Child Award'. The organizers announced that the International Child Peace Award will be conferred on her at The Hague, in the Netherlands in September 2013.

In the meanwhile, Malala received a letter from Adnan Rashid, a Taliban commander. He tried to say in it that he was not against girls' education. Here are a few extracts from the letter:

"Dear Malala Yousafzai,

"May God shower blessings on you.

"I heard about you for the first time on the BBC Urdu. I wanted to write you at that time itself and wanted to advise that you should stop writing against the Taliban. You might not know that we both belong to the same Yousafzai tribe, so I have sentiments related to you.

"I don't want to be involved in the debate whether the Taliban attack on you is justified or not.

"Malala, be assured that you have not been assaulted for your education. The Taliban and the Mujahiddin are not against education for boys and girls. I want to tell you that once the Indian subcontinent was highly educated, and every citizen could read and write before the English attacked. The local people taught the British officers Arabic, Hindi, Urdu and Persian. Not only this, the Muslim rulers spent a lot of money on education. There was no divide on matters related to poverty or religion because the educational system was based on great ideas and great curriculum.

"Malala, I want to draw your attention to Sir T.B. Macaulay's statement about what type of education he intended to impart in the Indian subcontinent. In his recommendation to the British Parliament on 2 February 1835, he said: "We have to create...ruled by us. The people who are Indians by blood and colour of their skin but are English by habits...intelligence."

"Malala, you must understand that this is the same so-called educational system for which you are ready to die.

"Look, Malala, the sense of mercy that you learnt from Prophet Mohammad, would the Pakistani army too had learnt then they must have stopped shedding Muslims blood. The sense of mercy that you have learnt from Jesus Christ must also be learnt by the American and NATO troops too. I wish to entreat the same thing to the followers of the Buddha that they must stop killing innocent and armless Muslims in Burma.

"I wish that the Indian Army should learn the same thing from Mahatma Gandhi.

Yours well-wisher
Adnan Rashid

This letter from Adnan Rashid to Malala came nine months after the assault, that was on 12 July.

A Milestone

On 12 July, it was Malala's birthday. She was especially invited to the UN headquarters at New York to address a youth assembly. The speech delivered by her on this occasion was telecast the world over. She presented her views forcefully before the delegates from all the countries of the world. She appealed for free education for all children in the world. In the main chamber of the UN, she was given the seat which is generally reserved for the heads of nation or government. At the time when Ban Ki Moon was describing her as 'our champion, our hero', she listened to him silently. When it was turn for her to speak, she said thus:

"At first, I take the name of omniscient, omnipotent and kind God. The honourable General Secretary of the UN Ban Ki Moon, honourable chairman of the General Assembly Wook Zeremik, the UN world education envoy honourable Gordon Brown, all senior respectable members, my brothers and sisters, today I get an opportunity to speak after a long interval. It is a matter of pride for me to be among so many respectable people, and this moment would remain etched in my memory for all times to come. I fail to understand wherefrom to start my talk, but I wish to thank all-powerful God for we all are equal, and then I thank all those who have prayed for my life. I cannot express in words the affection that people have showered on me. I have received cards and gifts from all over the world, and I thank everybody for these. I am also grateful to all those children whose innocent words have always motivated me. I also wish to thank all those senior people whose prayers have strengthened me. I thank all those nurses, doctors, hospitals in Pakistan and Britain and the UAE Government whose assistance and treatment enabled me to recover. I fully support the General Secretary Ban Ki Moon and envoy Gordon Brown for running the UN programme of Global Education First Initiative Programme. Besides, I also thank them for their leadership. I am hopeful that they will continue to inspire us all to work like this.

"My brothers and sisters, please keep one thing in the mind that Malala Day is not my day, it is a day for all those women and children who have raised their voice for their rights. Today there are numerous human rights organisations in the world, that are working for peace, equality and educational rights. Thousands of people are killed in the world each year in terrorist attacks, and millions others are injured. I am one of them, so I stand here, one of those girls.

"I am not speaking for myself, but for all boys and girls. I have not raised my voice to make a noise, rather I want to become the voice of all those people whose call goes unheard, who fight for their rights, who want the right to live peacefully, who want to have the right to live with equality and respect, who want right to education. Dear friends, the Taliban assailant, on 9 October 2012, shot me on the left temple, he shot my friend too; he thought that our voices could be silenced by their bullets, but they have direly failed. After this, thousands of voices emerged from the silence. Terrorists thought that I would deviate from my goal by this act of theirs, however, they could slaughter only infirmity, fright and despair of my life; their cowardly act has only infused determination and energy in me.

"I remain the same Malala, I still have the same goal which I had before the assault, and I am equally hopeful and optimistic, even today I am working courageously to fulfil my dream. Dear brothers and sisters, I am opposed to none, neither Taliban nor any other terrorist group, nor have I come here to discuss any enmity or revenge. I have come here to talk about the right to education for every child. I only want that the right to education should be availed by all people of the world.

"The children of Taliban and other terrorists must be given education in specific. I don't hate those terrorists who shot me. If they came before me while I had a loaded gun in my hand, I would not shoot them. I have learnt mercy from Prophet Mohammad, and this learning I have got from reading Jesus Christ and Lord Buddha. I have learnt the same tradition from Martin Luther King Jr., Nelson Mandela and Mohammad Ali Jinnah. Mahatma Gandhi, Bachcha Khan and Mother Teresa too had the same principles. I have learnt to forgive from my parents. My inner-self urges me to possess affection in the heart and be peaceful.

"Dear brothers and sisters, we can understand the value of light only when we are in the dark. We know the value of sound when we are in silence. The same way, when we were in Swat in northern Pakistan, we heard bomb explosions and gunfire on daily basis, and then we felt how essential books and pens are. There is an adage: A sword cannot hold before a pen. This remains true. The terrorists were scared of my pen and books; they were terrorized of the might of education, to the extent that they were scared of a woman. A woman's voice terrorized them. This is the reason that they killed fourteen innocent medical students in Quetta recently. For the same reason, they have killed many of my women teachers and polio workers in Khyber Pakhtunwah and Fata. They are destroying one or the other school daily. Education can bring about transformation and equality. Respectable General Secretary Sir, peace is essential for education. In many parts of the world, especially in Pakistan and Afghanistan, children cannot go to school owing to terrorism. We are tired of such a war.

"Women and children are desperate and resourceless in many parts of the world. In India, children are engaged in child labour. Many schools in Nigeria have been destroyed. People are suffering from extremism in Afghanistan. Little girls are employed in child labour and domestic duties, they are married when they are still minors. In such countries, both women and men suffer from poverty and penury, illiteracy and ignorance, injustice and racial discrimination, and they are deprived of human and basic rights. Dear friends, my focus is on women's rights and girls' education, because they suffer the most. There was a time when women social workers wanted cooperation of men for their rights, but today, they are working on their own. I don't mean to say that men should not talk of women's rights; what I mean to say is that women need to be independent and self-dependent to enjoy their rights and freedom. Dear brothers and sisters, now is the time when we must raise our voice. Today, we urge all leaders in the world to adapt their policies favourable to peace and prosperity. We appeal to all leaders of the world to include women's and children's security in the basic rights.

"All those steps which are in contravention of women's dignity should be rejected. We appeal to all governments in the world to make child education compulsory. We also appeal to them that they must fight against terrorism and violence, and all cruelty meted out to children must be stopped. All developed countries are expected to further expand educational opportunities for girls. We wish to tell all communities to initiate steps to end separation and inequality on the basis of caste, religion, region and sex. If even half of us lagged behind, we would not be able to advance at all. I would like to say to all my sisters that they must become brave and identify their abilities.

"Dear brothers and sisters, we need education and school for bright future of every child in the world. This journey of ours cannot be accomplished until there is provision of education for everybody. No one can obstruct us now. We will keep raising our voice for our rights, and on its basis, will bring about the change. For this, we will have to keep faith in the power of our words. Only this will change the world. We all are one and together for education. If we wish to realize our goal, we will have to equip ourselves with learning and unity.

"Dear brothers and sisters, we will have to remember that millions of people all over the world are victims of poverty, injustice and ignorance. We must not forget that millions of children are still out of the school. We must not forget that our brothers and sisters are awaiting bright and peaceful future. Come, let's pick up pens and books against illiteracy, poverty and terrorism; because these are the weapons with which we can fight these three. A child, a teacher, a pen and a book can change the world. Education is the only solution, so education must come first."

The noise that was caused due to the roar of claps echoed in the hall for long, and if her speech could bring only one thought in each mind. The terrorists must have thought of changing her intention, depriving her of the goal, but nothing had changed in Malala's life, rather all her infirmities, terror and desperation had been vanished, and she now stood with renewed might, strength and courage. It is simply beyond imagination what Malala as a little girl did. The news reports tell us that at the mere age of eleven years, Malala had urged the special envoy of America in Pakistan to use America's power and influence for curbing the Taliban's campaign against girls' education. Malala can work for girls' education all over the world, but the girls in Pakistan and Afghanistan need her all the more, as the Taliban continues to oppress innocent girls, much like it had happened with her.

On a pleasant sunny morning in September, the famous British artist Jonathan announced that he would make a portrait of Malala. He said: "It is a matter of honour for us to paint the most inspiring personality of our times." In the portrait that he made, Malala has been shown doing her homework. After this, it was decided that this picture would be displayed along side the pictures of Damien Hurst and Kevin Spacey, which too have been made by the same artist.

It was a matter of honour for Malala for her portrait to find a place in the National Portrait Gallery, and it touched her heart deeply. Jonathan said why he decided to sketch her portrait: "At that crucial turning of Malala's life, it was a matter of luck for me to spend time with her and her family. Despite all the struggle she faced, I did not take much time to understand that she was still a delicate adolescent. It is hoped that this painting could depict this paradox to some extent; in which she possesses indomitable energy and intelligence, while on the other she is delicate and young."

After this, there seemed to be in progress some sort of competition to honour her. On 27 September, 2013, Malala was conferred with the 2013 Peter J. Gomes Humanitarian Award at Harvard. The chancellor of the Harvard said that he was greatly pleased to honour her as she is a supporter of education. Malala was jointly honoured with American singer and human rights and social worker Harry Belafonte with the Ambassador of Conscience Award 2013 by the Amnesty International. On this occasion, Malala said that she wants to become a leader because a politician can influence the society on a large scale.

The Canada government decided to confer on Malala the honorary citizenship. This announcement was made on 16 October, 2013. This made Malala only the sixth individual to attain Canada's honorary citizenship. This honour in the past had been given to only the South African leader Nelson Mandela, the Nobel Peace laureate Aung San Suu Kyi, the Tibetan spiritual leader Dalai Lama, the British businessman Agha Khan and the Swedish politician Roil Wallenberg.

Anna Politkovaskaya, a human rights worker and journalist working against Chechnya conflict, was assassinated in Moscow on 7 October, 2006. On this day in 2013, Malala was conferred with Anna Politkovaskaya Award for her courage and giving voice to women and girls. On this occasion, the organizer said that Malala refused to be silent when the Taliban imposed its ban on girls going to school, just like Anna Politkovaskaya had done. He said that this was the reason that Malala was being conferred with this award.

On this occasion, Malala said that Anna Politkovaskaya was a devoted journalist and human rights worker. She started movements on a number of topics. She talked on several such issues on which others dared not.

After this, the International Day of the Girl was observed in America. When Malala arrived in America on 14 October on this occasion, a meeting was arranged with President Barack Obama in his Oval Office. In this meeting, she stressed the need for education. She was right to say that the future generation could be secured only through a better system of education. This was the reason that she was being appreciated for her views, and as a supporter of hope.

In fact, Malala remains a heritage of the community. Unfortunately, many of her messages have been clouded under doubts and suspicions at her home. She has to face unnecessary enmity in place of help. It may be due to controversial mentality, or maybe the thinking that this would make Pakistan look aloof from Malala's international image. Before she got the Nobel Prize, a statement was issued by the Taliban in which it expressed pleasure over her not getting the Nobel, only to attract mixed reactions. Both despair and pleasure were felt. Malala's humanity and her unchecked messages are innocent. She repeatedly talks of Pakistan and its difficulties; she does not want to relinquish her identity of being a Pakistani.

In Pakistan, some people feel that Malala is a votary of the Western countries. Responding to them, she said in an interview with the BBC: "My father says that education is neither Oriental nor Western. Education is education, everybody has right over it. The truth remains that the Pakistani people have supported me. It makes it clear that they don't think I am Western. I am a daughter of Pakistan and I am proud to be a Pakistani. The day I was shot, there were people standing with the banner 'I am Malala', they never said 'I am Taliban'. They supported me and encouraged me to move ahead with my campaign for girls' education. They want to help every child in every country, which we too can do."

She further said in her interview: "For now, we shall begin with Pakistan, Afghanistan and Syria, especially because they are the most troubled ones and they need us the most. Later in life, I want to go in politics, I want to become a leader, I want to bring about a change in Pakistan. I want to become a Pakistani leader, because I don't want to become a leader of any developed country."

In the first meeting of the Global Citizenship Commission, held in October 2013 in the University of Edinburg, 16-year-old Malala demanded that her campaign for education should not suffer. She said before the 1000-strong crowd that she was not scared after the assault even. She said: "We will have to be united and work together. When I was attacked, I felt that I would not be able to continue with my campaign, but now I find Kaynat and Shazia standing with me, and they are not terrorized, we are not frightened. People are cooperating with us, and they are our greatest strength." This programme had been held by the combined efforts of Gordon Brown, New York University and Carnegie Trust.

After this function, she met with the British Queen at the Birmingham Palace in London, where she was conferred with the honorary postgraduate degree of the University of Edinburg. She was also conferred with the Carnegie Award for her contribution in education and women rights.

When she was given the degree, about 1000 people present in the hall rose to their feet to give her a standing ovation. The Queen was greatly impressed by her bravery. Before this meeting, she had talked to Wajid Shamsul Hassan, Pakistan's High Commissioner in Britain, about her health.

This function was important and memorable for Malala for the reason that she could meet those friends of hers who too had been wounded in the assault. Now, all three of them were studying in Britain. Shazia had been given an offer of scholarship of the Atlantic college in Wales, so she too came to Britain. It was their first meeting after the Taliban's attack. Malala said that her two friends at her side would further strengthen her campaign for universal rights. They were especially invited in this meeting as guests.

On this occasion, Malala said: "I have come here for the first time, and it is a fine experience to see Scotland. It is necessary for people to come together for realizing a goal, it is necessary to work together, and so I feel myself more powerful."

In November, when the *Time* magazine published 16 most influential adolescents of the world for 2013, Malala's name found a place in it. This list also included the name of Malia, daughter of President Obama of America. This list comprises the names of young singers, players, talented children in the field of science and technology, writers and media icons, who become a source of inspiration for youths in the world owing to their work, motivation and extraordinary achievements.

Malala had got right from the nomination for the Nobel Peace Prize to the Sakharov Prize for Freedom of Thought and Clinton Global Citizen Award. She discussed with President Obama about educational rights, she met with the Queen of England, and also addressed the UN General Assembly. This sixteen-year-old girl was being appreciated for her dreams, courage and foresight the world over.

The *Time* magazine said that she did not hide herself to

protect herself from this assault, rather she went on to raise her voice and the world has been listening too. After this list by the *Time,* an announcement was made to confer on her the International Equality and Non-discrimination Award which was given to her in the beginning of 2014. This information was given in a statement issued by the Anti-discrimination National Council in Mexico. It said that she was being given this award for her efforts for preservation of human rights, especially without any discrimination with regard to caste, race, age or sex, as well as her contribution in the struggle for girls' education.

To bring out her fame and contribution in the form of a book, an initiative was taken by Weidenfeld and Nicholson Company of Britain, that entered into a three-million-dollar deal. It was decided that the company would publish the book by the title *I am Malala*. It was decided that this book would be printed and sold outside London by Little, Brown and Company. Malala knew that this story did not belong to only Malala, rather it was a story of those over six million girls who remain illiterate as they are unable to go to school. She hoped that the people would be able to know through the book how girls had to face difficulties in getting education. Malala had got a new lease of life defeating death. It was the victory of her resolute willpower.

On 23 November 2014, this memoir on Malala was announced to be included in the curriculum of a top university in America. It was well known that this Pakistani adolescent girl had become a source of inspiration all over the world so the university took this decision. The George Washington University announced that the memoirs will be used to prepare curriculum material with the help of teachers and publishers.

This book is an account of Malala's efforts. It unfolds several hidden aspects of her life. Marry Elysburg, director of the Global Women Institute (GWI) of the university, said: "Malala's courageous campaign for girls' education is a source of inspiration for all people. It is a matter of honour for us to construct the curriculum material in the capacity of educational associate of Malala with Little, Brown and Company. This curriculum material would educate students, at the same time would encourage the voice that was raised in connection with these matters." This curriculum would study the effect of a woman's call to make other women aware of different topics including global womanhood, political extremism and youth activism, etc. It is a matter of pride to get such an honour from a university, though there is controversy about this book in Pakistan.

A union of private schools in Lahore, Pakistan banned the book *I am Malala* saying that it would adversely influence the ideological foundation of students. However, there are other such unions of private schools in Pakistan, who all do not hold the uniform views. According to Mirza Qasif Ali, chairman of the All Pakistan Private Schools Federation: "The board has read this book well, and after this, the federation has decided that there are several such things in the book which would not be appropriate for children. The Muslims are of the opinion that the books written by Salman Rushdie contain many such things which are not acceptable keeping Muslims' sentiments and aspirations. And if Malala claims that Salman Rushdie has freedom to express himself then this statement would not have positive impact on children. Two women's witness is considered equal to one man's witness. It is not a matter of argument. It is part of our faith. It is a God's command. This style of writing raises doubts. The children who accept her as the role model are yet immature to understand all these things. We feel that it is not right to bring our children under her views. We don't want to be involved in any controversy in schools, so we have banned this book." Anyway, the fundamentalists in Pakistan might continue to thump their chests, but Malala had already become a global ambassador for children's rights.

The same week, the European Union awarded her with the prestigious Sakharov Human Rights Award. The chairman of the Union presented this award to her. Malala dedicated this award to all those unknown heroes of Pakistan and world's human rights workers.

She said on this occasion: "I hope that the EU would look towards the countries outside Europe, where people are still deprived of their basic rights, whose freedom of expression is being repressed." This award worth 65,000 dollars is considered the highest human rights award. It became still higher for her because it had been earlier awarded to Nelson Mandela and Aung San Suu Kyi too.

Looking at her contribution in educating girls and arming them with rights, she was selected, in November, for the Champion for Global Change Award, conferred by the United Nations Association of the USA. This was presented to her on 6 November 2013. Nine women, including Malala and pop singer Lady Gaga were honoured with the Glamour Women of the Year Award 2013. The presence of even Hollywood stars and Hillary Clinton, former foreign secretary, seemed to be lustreless before Malala. This award is given to the women who become a source of inspiration for other women. She was conferred The Girls' Hero for her campaign for changing the world. Besides, some money was also given to the Malala Fund too. This Fund is utilized for girls' education in the world.

In fact, it seemed to prove right what Malala said: "I suppose that the power of the pen is far more than that of a gun. In fact, a gun has no power, it can only kill people, but a pen gives life to man."

By December 2013, Malala became a celebrity whose statements were taken by the media readily and seriously. When in December 2013, Malala issued a condolence message on the death of Nelson Mandela, it was reported the world over. Describing Nelson Mandela, former President of South Africa, as her role model, she said: "He is an inspiration for all people of the world. He might have parted with us physically, yet his spirit and inspiration would continue to live on. He belongs to the entire world. He is a symbol of equality, freedom, love and such values which we need at all the times and places. His long struggle is an example for humanity. I have learnt much from him, he is my role model, he is an inspiration for me and millions others in the world."

Malala was thoughtful enough to think about even those children who were affected by the war. She visited Syria on behalf of the UN for the sake of children in the region in Syria-Jordan who had lost everything as consequent to the ongoing war from 2011. After she met Syrian children in the refugee camps in Jordan's desert area, she said: "When I saw children without education there, it hurt me deeply. They were running about barefoot in dirty lanes." The civil war was on in Syria, due to which people were forced to flee from there. In this camp located in neighbouring Jordan, about one lakh and a quarter people lived in deplorable condition, of which about 50,000 were sixteen years or less.

After her meeting with children there, she said: "I have seen terrorism in my Pakistan. Schools have been bombed and children killed. I can see a similar condition in Syria too. Children are being killed, many children had not gone to school for the past three years."

After the conflict started in Syria in 2011, over two million people have fled the country, they are forced to live in neighbouring countries of Jordan, Turkey and Iraq. According to the UN statistics, half of these refugees are children, and three-quarter of them are aged twelve years or below. An organisation concerned with the UN refugees, said that the children are very severely affected by the war. They are being brought up in broken families, they are away from education, and are compelled to live in dangerous situations. According to the UNHCR, many children have to work to earn a livelihood for their families. In Jatari, there are about 680 small shops being mostly run by children.

Though the UN is running a school here and giving them facilities to play, yet the children say that they have to face much difficulty in attending school as they have to walk long. The orthodox families put more restrictions on girls. Malala also visited a football ground under the care of the UN and met children there. She said: "The world ought to know the condition of these children. I myself have experienced these situations. It is hard to live away from home."

Malala said that she would run a campaign for the Syrians. For now, she wants to aid them from the Malala Fund. She wants to employ some teachers and get a school in Amman, Jordan repaired to resume studies there.

During her tour of Jatari, Malala asked a Syrian girl named, Jijon Malihan to accompany and help her in the camp. Five hours later, Jijon said: "I liked her greatly, we became like sisters."

In her charity work, Malala also included collecting funds. When in June 2014 it was reported that the Boko Haram, a Nigerian terrorist group, had kidnapped over 200 girls, a special fund was started by the Malala Fund. She said: "When I heard that the terrorists have kidnapped more than 200 girls, I was shocked. I am very concerned for these innocent girls, my sisters. Their only crime was that they were going to school and getting educated." Expressing grief over this incident, she said that the people of Nigeria should raise their voice against this incident, keeping mum would only encourage the terrorists to undertake such events in the future too.

She said: "We must speak else such incidents will keep occurring. The kidnapped girls are like our sisters. The Boko Haram must read the Quran because it teaches peace and brotherhood, and not violence and hatred."

In this connection, Malala decided to sell her portrait to donate the funds to the charity organisations in Nigeria for girls' and women's education. This portrait had been made by Jonathan when she had started attending the school in Birmingham.

The Christies, well known for putting famous articles to auction, presented Malala's this portrait for auction. It was being guessed that it would fetch somewhat sixty to eighty thousand dollars, but it was a craze among buyers, and it went for as high as 1,02,500 dollars within minutes.

Recently, Malala has raised her voice against *Khatna* (circumcision) for women. She has supported for the movement against female genital mutilation. Now she has also linked this issue with her global movement for educational rights for every girl; she is working to spread awareness on this account with the help of other adolescent friends.

In an interview with the *Guardian*, Malala admired the campaign led by the seventeen-year-old Fahima Mohammad and urged for better education in schools. She said: "I watch Fahima's movement in all its stages and I think she is doing such a massive work at such a young age. In recent times, more than one hundred and forty million girls and women have been mutilated. Moreover, in Pakistan, girls are kept aloof from education. In such a case, we have to face stiff challenges for a better new generation. I am like her sister and I am with her."

The Taliban, scared of Malala's campaign, has numerous forms. It changes its name and flag with a change in boundaries, but it retains its selfsame character, that is to keep women enslaved.

Is it not strange that women in the Muslim society lead in raising a voice for reform? It is the fearless voice of women right from Pakistan, Bangladesh to Iran, Saudi Arabia, or even reformative America and Europe. This stresses the need for rethinking on the Islamic way of living, thinking and traditions. Therefore, Malala cannot be accepted as an exception. There are numerous similar voices such as those of Ayyan Hirsi Ali, Wafa Sultan, Asra Nomani, Mukhtaran

Mai, Amina Vadud, Mona Eltahavi, Noni Darvesh, Basma bin Saud and others. We cannot reject them as ignorant, anti-Islam and American agents. If not today, the Muslim leaders, Ulemas and Alims will have to think about this seriously tomorrow. How long can you keep somebody mum on the force of threat or violence?

In fact, the semi-aristocratic and farming communities, the fundamentalist elements are terrorized of women's education because an educated woman becomes a challenge over private property and power. Therefore, they try to regulate women's education and hobbies in the pretext of religion, culture and tradition. Their Panchayats issue dictums that women can study, but not at all beyond religious books. They must not wear jeans and talk on mobile. It would be self-illusory to think that the women would remain free, respected and secure even in the capitalist society. The capitalist society seems to give educational, freedom and property rights to women at the initial stages, yet they are moulded very wilily, and they are reduced to something like a 'facility' for men. Freedom of body and sex is reduced to become a background for

prostitution. Fashion and aesthetics are so formulated that women are turned into showpieces, even to the extent that their motherhood rights are snatched away; and the matter of surprise is all about this is that women still feel that they are living freely. In the semi-aristocratic society, a woman thinks the zenith of her womanhood in *jauhar* or self-immolation, while in a capitalist society, she finds meaning in her becoming like a man. Women will have to guard against being an object. In sum, this is a conspiracy for sole rights over power and property. Therefore, the first condition for freedom of women lies in the destruction of semi-aristocratic structure in the society.

In a UN programme of development to fight against poverty, Malala said that her raising voice has brought a change in the lives of girls in the Swat valley in Pakistan who were earlier not allowed to go to school. Therefore, I urge you to raise prominently an issue which you confront.

She said: "Beyond fame, we all are alike. We may belong to a developed and rich country, or a developing and poor country. We all must have trust in ourselves. We all are capable, we all are special, so we all must work hard and start a movement for change."

Now, Davis Guggenheim, an Oscar award winner, is about to make a documentary on Malala. He won an Oscar in 2006 for a documentary titled *An Inconvenient Truth*. He said that its name was not yet final, though he said that the film would be ready by the year end. He said that there are few stories which are so powerful and significant as that is of Malala and her father Ziauddin. Whatever she did, she never thought that it would make her popular or she would get awards for that. However, when she sees so much being gifted by God, she is overwhelmed at so much respect after she evaded death by God's blessings.

It is said that extraordinary situations only bear extraordinary people. You might remember that Malala carries in her veins the blood of the same Pashtun tribe the people of which never compromise with their freedom. It is very troublesome to think that the entire generation is going to be enslaved. We cannot think of an entire generation deprived of education, basic rights, to be cast in unfathomable dark, in a generation where women would have no rights. It would be better to die than to live in such a condition.

There is no doubt that the women who raise their voices are being threatened. These women have been attacked not only in Muslim countries, but also in England, America, India and Canada. Still, they are coming out fearlessly, like Malala, in order to awaken the conscience of their communities.

Today, the Taliban can once again kill Malala but the warrior girl says: "They can shoot my body, but it is beyond their power to shoot down my dreams. They can kill Malala, but they cannot kill my goals. My goal is to light the flame of education, which could enlighten the world. Today, people encourage me on the Twitter, they motivate me for my goal. I have much to do yet, and I will keep working for that. My real award will be to get every child his right to education. I will struggle to get that award and work hard for this purpose."

The woman has yet to fight a long battle in both semi-aristocratic and capitalist societies for her human rights. It is evident that the new avatar of energy in the form of Malala would continue to reign.

□

9
Nobel Prize Award

A yet another hurt was caused by Malala to all organisations like the Taliban and those working in its style when she was given the Nobel Peace Prize. Though she had been nominated for the previous year's Nobel too, yet she could not get it, then it was given to an institute called OPCW which fights against the chemical weapons.

Malala's sixteenth birthday was celebrated in the UN. She became only the second person in history after Nelson

Mandela, whose birthday was celebrated in the UN. On this occasion, two prominent world leaders, Gordon Brown and Ban Ki Moon were present. She addressed the General Assembly at this time (we have already discussed this in the preceding pages).

Singers and musicians from over thirty countries sang songs to celebrate her birthday. This sixteen-year-old daughter of the Yousafzai tribe was given a three-million-dollar royalty, and she also got assistance from Cameroon, Ban Ki Mon and Hillary to gather funds for the Shakira Education Society. Her photograph appeared on the front page of the *News Week* and *Time*. With this, her name was included in the list of one hundred most influential people of the world. About two million children of the world proposed her name for the Nobel Prize with their signatures. As a result, the Norwegian Nobel Committee, on 5 December 2014, announced that Malala would be conferred with the Nobel Prize for Peace along with India's child rights activist Kailash Satyarthi (60).

Malala guessed that she could get the Nobel, but it was yet to be officially confirmed. The time for this confirmation was estimated when she could have been attending a class in school, so it was arranged that she would be told about this by the school administration during the chemistry class at ten in the morning on 5 December. Malala did not have a mobile phone, so her teacher said that she would come back at ten to the class to intimate any such thing. That day, Malala was studying about electrolysis of copper. And then it was quarter past ten. Disappointed, Malala thought that she was too young for a Nobel, her work is still in its formative stage, so she might not have got it. However, the teacher came a few minutes later, and broke the news in front of the entire class. At that time, Malala felt that her teachers were more enthusiastic than her. They had broader smile than her. Her classmates started to congratulate her, which she gleefully accepted. And after this, she went to attend her physics class like on other days. However, as soon as she went home, she got busy to prepare for her flight for Norway, where 10 December was awaiting her.

The names of Malala and Satyarthi were announced as the Nobel Prize winners from amongst 278 nominations, including 47 organisations. Getting the Nobel from amongst such well-known personalities was a unique feeling for Malala. Her innocence and attachment to education can be understood from the fact that despite this award, she continues to be eager for the school examinations that were soon to be held. As the youngest Nobel Prize winner, Malala passed the eve of the award ceremony watching a programme on a Pakistani television channel with her father in her Birmingham home. Speaking to the media, she said: "I am having cold and am not feeling well." She also expressed: "I wish that the Prime Ministers of both countries be present at the ceremony." However, this could not be realized. On the eve of the ceremony, she said: "If we teach children lessons of tolerance, patience and peace, God will bless good relations between India and Pakistan, and they will be like brothers once again. If children in India and Pakistan get education, their relations will automatically improve."

The sound of clapping in Oslo on 10 December 2014 resounded in both India and Pakistan. The Nobel Prize ceremony had never been so magnificent and memorable for Asian countries before, for India and Pakistan found themselves engaged in the same goal.

The president of the Norway Nobel Committee said in his address that Satyarthi and Malala were certainly the people whom Alfred Nobel, in his will, termed as messengers of peace. He further said that a girl and an old man, a Pakistani and an Indian, a Muslim and a Hindu, both of them are symbols of unity which the world needs today, brotherhood between these two countries is needed today. Ironically, this joint Nobel prize was being given to an Indian and a Pakistani at a time when the border between the two countries witnessed severe tension.

The President of the committee further said that no faith holds violence and repression justifiable. All of Islam, Christianity, Jainism, Hinduism and Buddhism protect life, and cannot be used for taking away life. He further said that they were there to honour two people who have proved themselves true to this point. They live according to the principle which was expressed by Gandhiji. He had said: "There are many objectives for which I can give my life, but there is none such for which I can take somebody's life."

In the award ceremony, the popular Pakistani singer Rahat Fateh Ali Khan and the well-known Indian musician Amzad Ali Khan displayed their skills. The former Prime Minister of Pakistan Yusuf Raza Gilani too was present here. The Nobel Peace Prize was given in the presence of Emperor Herold V and Queen Sonja, representatives of the Norwegian government, Parliament and other guests by the President of the Norwegian Nobel Committee. Both Satyarthi and Malala got the Nobel medal, made from 18-carrot green gold, covered with 24-carrot gold water, each weighing 175 gm. The medals were designed by Gustav Vigeland of Norway. The two winners shared 1.1 million dollars, or about seven crore rupees each.

Malala became the first Pakistani and the youngest ever person to get this award. While accepting the award, Malala said that she was proud to be a Pakistani and wished that peace should prevail everywhere. She thanked her father for not having clipped her wings and let her fly freely. She thanked her mother who told that Islam tells to speak the truth always.

She said: "I dedicate this award to all those children whose voice is needed to be heard. For this honour is not for me, rather it is for those forgotten children who want to study; it is for those terrified children who want peace; I am here to raise their voices. I am a form of those sixty-six million girls who have not been fortunate enough to get education.

"This award is for those children who want change in the world. I and Kailash Satyarthi can stand together and show to the world that we can be united for the children's rights in India and Pakistan and establish peace. This faith can be expressed only by a child, the grown-ups have taken politics as the fate.

"This year also observes one hundred years of the First World War; however, we have failed to learn a lesson. Many parts of the country still witness warlike situations, including Iraq, Gaza, Syria, Afghanistan and Pakistan too. Many children in Africa cannot go to school because of poverty. In India and Pakistan, many children are deprived of schooling owing to social prohibitions.

"I am an individual who is stubbornly committed to my goal, so I want that every child must get education. I am not a voice in isolation, rather I am many voices together. It is easier to give gun to a hand, but it is hard to give it book."

Advocating girls' education, Malala said that neither terrorists, nor their bullets could snatch away her intentions. She said: "I want equal rights for all women in the world, and also want that there is peace in every corner of the world. I firmly believe in Islam, which gives a message of peace; unfortunately, there are people who know little about this faith. I accept that all are humans, and they should be friendly to one another. There are borders between countries, but it never means that we should hate one another. India and Pakistan should work together in the fields of education and development. We will work together and try to strengthen relations between India and Pakistan. It is more essential to work for progress and development rather than for war."

Stressing the need for children's education, she said that change could be brought through this. She said that the Swat valley witnessed change only through this, people will have to struggle for their rights.

People have felt that Malala is a wonderful orator even at the small age of seventeen years. Sometimes, she raised her voice as if to give the effect of awakening people from their slumber.

Malala has donated the money from the Nobel Prize to the Malala Fund. Doing this, she said that this money would be utilized for girls' education.

As always, Malala and Satyarthi were given the Nobel Prizes at the Stockholm Concert Hall, the most attractive point of which is the Nobel Museum. It preserves the objects donated by the Nobel Prize winners. Tourists, especially students, visit this museum round the year. According to the director of the museum: "The present museum spreading over one thousand square metres is smaller for the present needs; we are not able to display many of those objects owing to shortage of space."

Malala donated one of her dresses to this museum. It was displayed in the Nobel Peace Prize exhibition, she had worn it when she was attacked by the Taliban. It has been done so on her insistence. It was for the first time that Malala's blood-soaked school dress was before the world, and she could not hold her tears on seeing it. Seeing tears in her eyes, Kailash Satyarthi comforted her and said: "You are very brave."

No doubt, Malala is the epitome of bravery; this honour is a symbol of inspiration for the entire world. Her selection for this peace prize is a severe hurt for terrorism and those who want to keep girls away from education. This time was considered very vital as far as discouraging terrorism in the world is concerned.

For now, people are once again focussed on issues pertaining to childhood as well as relations between India and Pakistan. It remains in the garb of future what the joint mission by Malala and Satyarthi will bear in the future, but the Nobel prizes to both of them have brought child labour, child slavery, children's sex exploitation, girls' education and other such important matters to the fore. There is an urgent need to blossom and nurture childhood, and this would be the greatest achievement of this award.

□

Timeline

1997 – Born on July 12.

2008 – Gave her first speech at the local press club in Peshawar, titled "How dare the Taliban take away my basic right to education?"

2009 – Started Blogs for the BBC under the name Gul Makai

2009 – Taliban issues edict against education. Malala writes that she continues to prepare for her exams.

2009 – Contributed to the show Capital Talk. Spoke out against the Taliban's decision to prevent women from accessing education.

2009 – Taliban lifts edict on women attending school.
Left her home because of Taliban's attack on Swat Valley. Met Richard Holbrooke for educational help. December 1, identity was released because of increasing publicity.
Nominated for International Children's Peace Prize at age 13

2011 – Won Pakistan's National Youth Peace Prize

2012 – Attacked by a Taliban gunman
October 12, Fatwa issued against the Taliban gunman.
October 15, UN Special Envoy for Global Education Gordon Brown started a petition to support Malala's dream. With the slogan "I am Malala", the petition aimed to ensure that every child would be in school by 2015.

Runner up for the 2012 TIME Person of the Year

2013 – Gave her first public speech at UN since the shooting. Her message was: "Our books and our pens are the most powerful weapons."

September 9, Nominated for the Nobel Peace Prize

October 8, 2013 her autobiography titled "I am Malala: The Girl Who Stood Up for Education and Was Shot by the Taliban" was released.

2014 – Awarded Nobel Prize for Peace

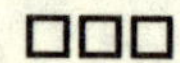